NEW JOB SURVIVAL KIT

10 STEPS TO SURVIVING AND THRIVING IN THE FIRST 100 DAYS OF YOUR NEW JOB

Frances Kay

Marshall Cavendish Business

Copyright © 2006 Frances Kay

First published as *New Kid on the Block* in 2006
This edition published in 2012 by Marshall Cavendish Business
An imprint of Marshall Cavendish International

1 New Industrial Road, Singapore 536196
genrefsales@sg.marshallcavendish.com
www.marshallcavendish.com/genref

Other Marshall Cavendish offices: Marshall Cavendish Corporation. 99 White Plains Road, Tarrytown NY 10591-9001, USA • Marshall Cavendish International (Thailand) Co Ltd. 253 Asoke, 12th Flr, Sukhumvit 21 Road, Klongtoey Nua, Wattana, Bangkok 10110, Thailand • Marshall Cavendish (Malaysia) Sdn Bhd. Times Subang, Lot 46, Subang Hi-Tech Industrial Park, Batu Tiga, 40000 Shah Alam, Selangor Darul Ehsan, Malaysia

Marshall Cavendish is a trademark of Times Publishing Limited

The right of Frances Kay to be identified as the author of this work has been asserted by him in accordance with the Copyright, Designs and Patents Act 1988.

All rights reserved

No part of this publication may be reproduced, stored in a retrieval system or transmitted, in any form or by any means, electronic, mechanical, photocopying, recording or otherwise, without the prior permission of the copyright owner. Requests for permission should be addressed to the publisher. The author and publisher have used their best efforts in preparing this book and disclaim liability arising directly and indirectly from the use and application of this book. All reasonable efforts have been made to obtain necessary copyright permissions. Any omissions or errors are unintentional and will, if brought to the attention of the publisher, be corrected in future printings.

A CIP record for this book is available from the British Library

ISBN 978-981-4382-34-2

Printed in Singapore by Fabulous Printers Pte Ltd

Marshall Cavendish publishes an exciting range of books on business, management and self-development.

If you would like to:
- Find out more about our titles
- Take advantage of our special offers
- Sign up to our e-newsletter

Please visit our special website at: www.business-bookshop.co.uk

Contents

Introduction   5

Step 1   7
Making a graceful exit

Step 2   21
Rising to new challenges

Step 3   38
Start as you mean to go on

Step 4   58
Getting and keeping yourself organized

Step 5   79
The importance of clear communication

Step 6   100
Being part of the team

Step 7 118
How to win friends and influence people

Step 8 140
Developing successful working relationships

Step 9 157
Dealing with problems

Step 10 175
Maintaining performance and ongoing development

About the Author 191

Introduction

You've just landed the most exciting job in a new company, or you've got that long-awaited promotion you'd been hoping for. Congratulations! Whichever it is, right now you're probably experiencing a wave of euphoria. But wait—what if this mood is shortly replaced by a feeling of apprehension and a little self-doubt? What then?

Don't worry: this is perfectly normal. Many people find it daunting or quite scary when facing an entirely new situation. Some of us may even admit to feeling somewhat inadequate and not quite confident that we're up to the task ahead.

Help is at hand. *New Job Survival Kit* gives you strategies for maximizing your strengths and taking advantage of the new opportunities coming your way. It will help you to create an inspiring work environment that fulfills your dreams and aspirations. You'll achieve this more easily when you give the right impression, make shrewd decisions, act wisely, and take appropriate steps during the first few months in your new role.

Jobs for life are rare these days, so being a "New Kid" is a situation most of us experience at least a few times, if not more often, during our careers. Each time we change job and move out of our comfort zone, we leave behind everything that is familiar. This can be frightening, even for those normally brimming with confidence. Immersed in new surroundings it is natural to feel insecure and nervous.

New Job Survival Kit is a step-by-step guide. It is designed to take you through:

- Making the right first impression
- Developing good relationships with your boss, colleagues, and staff
- Learning the ropes
- Ringing the changes, if necessary

Starting as you mean to go on It shows you that with sensible thought, good preparation, planning, and some self-discipline you can do more than just survive the first few months in your new job; you could even enjoy the experience!

Frances Kay

Step 01

So Long, Farewell, Auf Wiedersehen, Adieu: Making A Graceful Exit

> **❝** Goodbye. I am Leaving because I am bored. **❞**
>
> *George Saunders*

Well done! You've achieved your goal, and won that coveted new position. New horizons are opening up before you. What are the most important things to consider before taking up your new appointment? Pause for a moment, retrace a few steps in order to reflect and prepare your new game plan.

The moment you were offered your new position, and accepted it, it was obvious that much was about to change. Whether you are already in employment, are coming back into the workplace after a break, or are about to take up your first appointment, your attitude toward your current employer, situation, or place of learning probably changed dramatically. You began to let go emotionally from your current position. Although still important to you, it was no longer the primary focus point.

As a student you might have begun thinking about salary checks arriving promptly each month in your bank account. If you've been unemployed or absent from work for a while, you could be wondering what changes you'll need to make to your routine to work a five-day week.

Looking at the situation from an employee's viewpoint, you might have experienced mixed feelings about leaving your current position. Some people feel rather disloyal because they are excited about their future prospects. Unless you are desperately unhappy at work, you might be reflecting on the comparative ease with which you've fitted into your role. What are you doing, leaving everything familiar behind you and striking out into uncharted territory?

HANDING OVER THE REINS

> **!** Aim for as smooth and seamless an exit strategy as possible

While working out your notice you should, as a professional, continue to do a competent and conscientious job for your current employer. However, your mind may well be straying toward your new situation and the many things that are likely to change.

This transition stage between the old, familiar job and the new position is a tricky one. Many factors come into play, which can throw up issues of loyalty and responsibility. Notice periods can sometimes be fraught and stressful, and where there is awkwardness at work a month can seem a very long time indeed.

How you work out your notice is likely to be dictated by the terms of your contract, your relationships within the company, what sort of job you have, and how senior you are. Many people are obliged to give a month's notice. If the position you hold is a more senior one, your firm may require a longer period—perhaps three months or more. It could even be a year, particularly if finding a suitable replacement for you is likely to be a difficult or lengthy procedure.

On the other hand, depending on circumstances, it may be possible to negotiate a "quick getaway." It's not advisable to choose this route if you have to push your boss into agreeing to it. But if they're not opposed to it, it could be advantageous and, provided it's financially viable, could give you a useful breather between your old and new job.

It's important to bear in mind what the issues are here. Your boss's main concern will be to avoid difficulties of handover. For instance, have you been handling complex projects? Are they coming to an end? Do you have colleagues willing—and able—to oversee them once you have left? How quickly is your replacement likely to take up their post? All these factors will be uppermost in your employer's mind, and the more of them you can identify, help to control, or offer possible solutions for, the greater your chances of shortening your notice period.

What preparation are you able to make to smooth the transition from you to your successor? Have you, for instance, been making progress notes or critical path analyses if involved in complex projects? Has someone already been chosen to replace you? Is it an internal appointment—in which case are they being given time to shadow you while you're still in post? Are they able to take advantage of any in-house training schemes that will prepare them for taking over from you?

If an external candidate is replacing you, have you met them? Is their past experience relevant to the new post? Will they already be familiar with most of the tasks it entails? Have they had similar responsibilities in their previous job? Offer to spend a few days or a week with them as a handover period.

> John recently left the advertising agency where he had been an accounts executive. He arranged for his replacement to come into the office and spend his last week with him, learning the ropes sitting beside him. This is how he planned it.
>
> During the first two days John showed his successor, Stuart, exactly what he did and how things were handled in the office. "I covered everything," John said, "right from which way to put the paper in the printer to the style of report needed for the executive board meetings." Stuart was able to see it all "live," and gained a much clearer picture watching John in action. The second two days John sat beside Stuart at his desk and made sure he started working on the client accounts right away. With John supporting him and providing information if he was stuck, Stuart was able to manage quite well. On the fifth and last day, John removed himself to an empty office. He had

> plenty of things to finish off and clear away. Stuart had "taken over" his role and was seen by the other staff to be established in post.

Whatever the situation—and there are endless variations—the more helpful you are to your employer, your organization, and your colleagues, the more likely you are to have a smooth handover.

You will probably be able to organize the timing and style of your departure to your mutual satisfaction and convenience.

GOODBYE OR AU REVOIR

Some human resources professionals within organizations like to interview leavers, just as they interview prospective employees. It's therefore possible that your company will require you to undergo an "exit interview." The purpose behind these is to attempt to find out firsthand why an employee is leaving, and whether anything could have been done to retain their services.

Another reason is to gain knowledge of the leaver's experience of working in the department or organization. It could, for example, be helpful in drawing up skills specifications and job descriptions for future employees. Discretion and tact is a prerequisite here. The more general and diplomatic you can be, the less likely there is to be "fallout" as a result of what you disclose. There is little advantage to "spilling beans" to the extent that you upset former colleagues. After all, who knows when or where you may meet them again. Even if the thought of "telling the unvarnished truth" about the boss from hell is tempting, it might not be helpful if you're in need of a decent recommendation.

When it comes to it, wouldn't we all prefer our leaving party to be full of colleagues who regard us with affection and express regret at our leaving, rather than viewing the event with relief and a feeling of "good riddance—I thought this day would never come!"

Unless it is standard practice in your company to mark staff departures with a formal occasion and presentation, it's probably sensible to arrange your farewell in an informal and friendly way. Most soon-to-be-ex-workmates are happy to say adieu over a few drinks at a local bar. It gives everyone an opportunity to express thanks for past favors and to acknowledge the time you've worked together.

After you've left you could even write to your former boss to say how much you enjoyed working with them (if it's not a blatant untruth), and to send your best wishes for the future to all your former colleagues. This isn't essential, but in these days of frequent job changing, why not smooth things along if you can? You never know—someone from your previous company may one day turn up at your new workplace. Isn't it better to be thought of positively rather than negatively?

Resigning or leaving with a professional and courteous manner enhances your professional reputation. The people you are leaving behind may be a rich source of contacts and recommendations for your future career prospects. They are far more likely to be willing to provide a recommendation or influence people on your behalf if they recall working with you as a pleasant experience, rather than with a shudder of revulsion.

By doing everything you can to facilitate a smooth handover for your successor—and that includes continuing to work conscientiously until your last day, not helping yourself to equipment, supplies, or reference material to which you are not entitled—you will go a long way toward achieving your aim. Thank colleagues and your former boss for all their support and you will be remembered favorably.

MANAGING THE CHANGEOVER

> ! If you cen, take a break between jobs.

So, you've served out your notice period, waved goodbye to former colleagues and boss, and are now on your way to taking up your new position. Have you planned a respite break between jobs? Don't you need a bit of time for yourself, to get your brain around the challenges ahead?

Harriet organized a long break for herself between jobs. She says that arranging to go on a three-month vacation after leaving her old job was the best thing she'd ever done. Admittedly she was in a senior position as a property professional and was able to plan her departure to suit both the organization and herself.

The plan she devised was booking a 12-week trip to the Far East to coincide with the end of her notice period, the end of the company's financial year, and—conveniently—the long Christmas and New Year period, when everything is quiet and few people are at their office.

This logical thinking on Harriet's part meant that her company was supportive of her exit strategy, and Harriet herself was able to leave with minimum stress. The trip not only fulfilled one of her ambitions, but also gave Harriet the opportunity to "wind down." Her successor was welcomed in post and had a much easier job of taking over from her after such a decisive "break point."

Harriet explained that she'd been doing a job where she was seen as "irreplaceable." Taking over from her would have been difficult for anyone, and she realized that, however competent her successor, it would be easy for him to feel that he was working in her shadow.

Because of the way she handled her departure, she not only had a memorable time, but her absence was long enough to enable her to distance herself from her

> previous responsibilities before taking up her current position. She told me that on her return from vacation she felt exhilarated, rested, fit, and a new person.
>
> The job she was moving to was also a highly responsible one and she knew that the first few months were going to be the steepest of learning curves. How sensible then for her to ensure that on arrival at her new company she was in good health and looking forward to meeting new challenges.

It may not be possible for all of us to replicate this situation, but it does seem sensible to try something along these lines. There's no way you'll present yourself well or be able to do your best work with a new boss and colleagues if you're stressed out and nervous as a result of what you've left behind.

Before you arrive at your new desk, you should try to negotiate a couple of weeks' break. If nothing else, it enables you to have "closure" on the previous position. You know how very busy people take at least a week to relax when they go on holiday. In fact, they can be a perfect nuisance for the first few days. They calm down in the middle of the vacation and then start winding up again as they prepare to return to work.

GETTING YOURSELF READY

Between jobs, there's a huge amount to do. You should try to give yourself a chance to relax, refresh, and regroup before embarking on your new position. Assuming that you have some time between jobs, how do you make the most effective use of it? Because I'm a bit of a list addict, I think it's essential to make a note of all the things that need sorting out.

There are a number I would mention—in no particular order of priority.

PERSONAL HEALTH

This is something that the company you're moving to may well have taken care of with your employment package. However, if you haven't been offered a full medical through the company scheme, it might be sensible to arrange a health check and a visit to the dentist before you start your new job. Of course, if you're in the process of some treatment already, take the opportunity to get any doctor or dental appointments out of the way now. In your first few weeks in your new position it will be far better to be able to give it your full attention than to have to ask for time off to attend clinics or other appointments.

DOMESTIC AFFAIRS

It may seem rather strange to include this subject, but is your house in good shape? If you've been struggling to find time to get the central-heating boiler checked out or the intruder alarm serviced, it would be sensible to get these seen to before returning to work. Few companies seem able to fix an appointment these days. The best you get is "sometime between 8 a.m. and 1 p.m." In your first few days in your new job it would look rather poor to ask for a morning off because the gasman is coming. So do a bit of planning, and if you have the time get your house in shape as well as yourself.

STYLE AND PRESENTATION
Is this too obvious to mention here? Not necessarily. So many of us find it difficult to juggle a busy career with home, social, and family life. When you're taking on a new position, isn't it a good plan to give your confidence a boost by knowing you look your best? Maybe you're not in a position to throw out your entire wardrobe and re-equip yourself with new clothes, but perhaps you should consider consigning one or two well-worn items to the thrift store? A haircut, a change in diet or life style? Whatever you think might make a difference, it's a good time to start new habits that will help improve image and enhance self-esteem.

FINANCES
This is an important consideration and well worth spending some time on. If you need to rearrange your finances, get this sorted out before starting your new job. For your own sake, it is vital to make sure that the human resources department has all your details correctly on file. If you're opening a new bank account or want to make arrangements regarding payment of your salary, give yourself time to get the correct forms filled out or letters sent giving authority for changes to be made.

SELF-ORGANIZATION

Now would also be the perfect time to review your paperwork, files, records, and contact information. Before starting your new job it might be worth while spending a bit of time checking that your contact information is up to date. If you've recently cleared your desk, you may well find that there are a number of boxes full to the brim with old paperwork and other items. Do you really need all of it? Are you proposing to lug it all over to your next place of work and then set about sorting through it at a convenient moment in your new employer's time? Best to take a critical view of it before you start your new job. If possible, be ruthless. You'll feel much better once you've tackled this. If these supposedly important pieces of information haven't seen the light of day for six months or more, you'll probably be able to do without most of them!

DOING A "RECCE"

Of course, the best thing to do before you start work at your new company is to undertake some thorough research on the organization. Take advantage of your preparation time to make as many inquiries as you can about all the things you'll need to know when you start your new job. Good research creates understanding and confidence, both of which will put you at an advantage when in a new situation.

By the time you were offered the job and had accepted it, you would have had some knowledge of the organization you are about to become part of. You probably attended at least two interviews and became familiar with the location of the office and the best means of travel to and from it. But before you actually take up your new position, you might want to continue fact-finding and researching.

Keep your eye on the press and on professional journals. See if your new company is in the news. Read articles about the sector, the industry, government policy, and related companies. You can learn a great deal from this kind of research. Not only will it help you familiarize yourself with the environment in which you'll be working, but you'll learn what factors are important and how they affect the organization.

How much do you really know about the company?

- Have you been able to obtain copies of the annual report and accounts?
- Do you have any of the brochures, or sales and marketing material?
- How often have you looked at their website?
- What information is available about the board of directors?
- Are their biographies available on the website? You'll find it useful if you're familiar with their names and recent progress.

If you were able to obtain other relevant information from your new employer, such as a company handbook or induction manual, it would be a good idea to study this prior to starting work. It will help you to feel more comfortable on your first day if you already have a rough idea of the way the company works and of its culture.

You were probably introduced to some of your future colleagues at your interviews. It's most likely that you'll have met your immediate boss. If you think it would be helpful, you could ask if it's possible to go in for a day, or part of a day, before you take up your position, in order to familiarize yourself with the layout of the office and meet one or two colleagues informally.

This will depend entirely on the type of organization and job you are moving to. Do be sensitive to your new organization. Some places are security conscious and would not permit a casual approach. Under these circumstances, it might be more appropriate to ask if a formal tour of inspection is customary.

For most companies it would probably be acceptable if you approached your new boss or departmental head and inquired about the viability of a familiarization visit. If by arranging your visit for lunchtime or late afternoon you could combine it with going for a drink with future colleagues, it would establish your friendly approach.

Enthusiasm, proactivity, and initiative will give you an advantage and create a positive relationship with your co-workers.

> There's never a second chance to make a first impression, so why not take the opportunity to come across well even before you've officially started?

STEP 02

New Brooms, New Kids, And New Pastures: Rising To New Challenges

❝Always take a job that is too big for you.**❞**

Anon

Are you worrying that as a New Kid you've bitten off more than you can chew? If you are, it shows that you're aiming high and have ambition. Your new job may well be a step (or two) up the ladder. This is a good thing. Don't be daunted, even though the role requires specific approaches and new skills. Adjustment will be necessary and this book is designed to help you settle into your new role quickly and effectively.

WHAT TO EXPECT

Don't underestimate the amount of change involved in the transition from your old job to your new one. Even if you've been promoted from within the same organization, your new role will almost certainly involve added responsibilities and challenges.

Here are a few points to bear in mind:

PRIVATE/PUBLIC SECTOR

If you're moving from the private to the public sector or vice versa, for example, the change in culture will be very marked. A big adjustment will be required to rise to the challenge of being a New Kid in a new working culture.

CULTURAL AND ETHNIC ISSUES

There is great cultural diversity in the modern workplace. Some New Kids will be from abroad or may not have English as their first language. Whatever your situation, make sure that your induction is appropriate to your needs. If you feel you need more time or training to become accustomed to your new working environment, don't be afraid to speak to your immediate supervisor or the HR director about it.

INDUCTION TRAINING

The first 100 days for a New Kid will vary considerably, depending on the level of seniority at which they enter the organization. As a junior New Kid you'll probably need more of an introduction and hand-holding period than a more experienced person. This should be the responsibility of your training manager or HR director. If you're not given adequate induction training, request this from your immediate superior.

Senior New Kids will probably have a formal "induction program." You may find that a number of "meet the people" events have been arranged. You could even have "free" accommodation for some months on arrival, particularly if you've relocated from far away. The induction timetable is adhered to until completed, by which time total absorption in the corporate culture and hierarchy should have taken place.

HOW DID YOU GET HERE AND WHY?

Think for a moment about how you landed this new job. Did you get it because you were particularly successful at what you used to do? Have you moved to a more senior position within the same company, or to a new one, doing broadly similar work, because you have outstanding experience? Or are you moving to a new position because of particular skills you have? Then consider how you are going to achieve the results you want in your new position.

Taking over a new position means three important things for all New Kids. They're probably the most important issues you'll have to face in your new job.

- Challenges: what are you looking for?
- Learning curves: how are you going to deal with them?
- Comfort zones: are there any aspects of the job that are friendly and familiar? A new job doesn't necessarily have any comfort zones, but it helps if you can find a few to get you through the first 100 days

One of the best ways to ensure you succeed in your new job is to have the right attitude. If you see your new role as something exciting, requiring different approaches from those you've used in the past, and offering you greater challenges, this is a healthy sign. Your prior experience will be necessary and useful, but by looking forward, trying to learn fast, you'll be showing the right attitude.

> **!** In the early days of your new job, keep an open mind. Suspend reaction, don't make assumptions and judgments, or jump to conclusions about systems, people, or projects.

You should consciously define and adopt new ideas and approaches. Your actions and attitude during the first few days and weeks in a new job can make the difference between success and failure.

You'll probably find that one of the main challenges of your new job is people—other people. You'll certainly have work of your own, which you may be able to do independently, but you may also be expected to work as part of a team, perhaps in an open-plan office where people are interacting all the time, and some of your responsibilities may require you to report directly to others, or to have staff reporting to you.

Working with and relating to new people requires effort; it takes time and expertise. There's much more to it than simply allocating tasks. It's important to remember that tasks can be learned, skills taught and acquired, relatively quickly. Results are what it's all about. But where people are concerned, while you'll need to find out about their attitudes and personalities swiftly and sensitively, getting to know them will be a long and often quite complex process.

GETTING DOWN TO WORK

Once in your new job, you will have identified your set of

key tasks. It's up to you to figure out how to get results. This will involve:

- Planning (what must be done to achieve the desired outcome)
- Organizing (yourself, time, other people, activities)
- Recruitment and selection (if managing a team or department)
- Training and development (of your own skills or those of your staff)
- Motivation (creating and maintaining a positive attitude)
- Control (monitoring your own performance standards and those of others)

Success as a New Kid will vary depending on the exact nature of the work you do. It's most likely that you'll be expected to be able to take decisions and make them work, as well as being adept at problem solving, time management, communication skills, and relationship building. It's essential to keep a clear head and an eye on both the detail and the bigger picture, as well as becoming expert in the skills your role demands.

SURVIVING THE FIRST FEW DAYS

Three things to help New Kids storm their way through the first few days:

- **Confidence**

  New Kids nearly always feel intimidated and overwhelmed at first. However, if you approach people and your work with confidence, letting colleagues know you're in control, they'll trust you. Courses on public speaking are a great way of learning to overcome shyness and to get your point across clearly

- **Knowledge**

    Knowing people's names is a great help. If in a position to do so, New Kids should identify the company's directors and other senior personnel and find out what their roles are. Quite a few company websites include a list of key personnel, and, if you're really lucky, the pages may include pictures. Once you're in post, if the company has an intranet, use it. It can be a great resource. Everything you need will probably be found on the intranet site. Have as much information as possible at your fingertips: internal phone directory, speed dialing codes, departmental electronic calendar, contact lists, useful phone numbers, operation manuals (for voicemail, telephones, etc.). If you think you'll need it, get trained in the appropriate IT packages—especially Word, Excel, and PowerPoint—so that your computer skills are strong

- **Networking**

    In the first couple of months, socialize as much as possible. Accept invitations to after-work drinks, lunches, and group events. Arrange coffees and lunches to get to know your immediate colleagues better. If time allows, volunteer to help with work events or corporate functions. The latter are particularly valuable if your job as New Kid involves working with clients. The better your interpersonal skills, the more likely you'll be to succeed in your role. It's a well-known fact that success in business is 20 percent strategy and 80 percent people. If you can communicate well with others (in business writing, giving presentations, running meetings, liaising with staff on a one-on-one basis, conducting interviews and appraisals), this will improve your chances of being effective sooner rather than later. This is a crucial starting point in any new job

Sometimes office space itself is an issue for New Kids.

Martin started work as a senior New Kid director three years ago. Until then, he says, he had never worked in an open-plan office. His initial reaction: "It sucks, I tell you! I would give anything to have an office back, a door to close, some privacy in which to work, and some quiet when holding a telephone conversation. Even the ability to exert control over the temperature in my personal space and to open a window and let the fresh air in, if I so choose. Is this too much to ask? What price a door? Just so that I can hang a notice on it saying, 'Please do not disturb.'"

However, Martin gradually got used to the new working environment and the effect was very positive. His staff related better to him and he had closer contact with colleagues than he had done in his previous office, where it was all too easy for him to retreat into

> his inner sanctum. With increasingly flexible working practices and less formal and hierarchical offices, New Kids would be well advised to settle into the new office ambience despite any initial misgivings.

FOCUS ON THE POSITIVE

Have you ever made a note of the skills you have and how you rate them? This sort of self-analysis is useful when in a New Kid situation. If you've ever received feedback in your previous jobs, you'll no doubt remember that it mostly accentuates the negative. Employee evaluations tend to focus on opportunities for improvement, the sting of criticism often lasting longer than the glow of praise.

Maybe it would be sensible at this stage to conduct a self-appraisal designed to give you an idea of your personal best. By raising your self-esteem, you'll be able to increase your future potential. There are probably a number of people who could help you do this. Collect some feedback from, say, six people who know you well—from both within and outside of work. Ask them only to provide information on your strengths.

When you've had their input, look at the results. What patterns are there? Are there any common themes? You could spend a little time organizing them into groups and themes, adding any of your own observations.

From this study, you should be able to compose a fairly accurate positive self-portrait. You should even be able to write a description of yourself that summarizes what you can achieve when operating at full capacity. Now compare this to your personal job description. The purpose is to concentrate on what you are good at and create a better fit between your work and your "best" self.

Your job description and profile set out the abilities required by the post. You obviously have most of these, otherwise you wouldn't have been given the job. Now you can discover who you are when at the top of your game. You can then look ahead to see if things could be improved, using your strengths to shape the way you work, and thereby controlling the next phase of your career. By taking action as a result of accurate self-appraisal, you'll be helping both yourself and your employer.

However, if there seems to be a skills weakness in a particular area and you feel that something should be done, try to organize some training as soon as possible. Most companies are helpful about such things, and one that cares about its employees will be supportive. If you take the time and trouble to analyze your strengths and identify where improvements could be made, you'll be regarded as an excellent New Kid.

FOCUS ON PRIORITIES

Whatever your job, you'll be subject to Pareto's Law (the 80/20 rule). This means that 80 percent of results flow from just 20 percent of causes. Make it personal: 20 percent of what you do contributes disproportionately to what you achieve.

This is important for everyone, but particularly for

New Kids. Your situation as a new recruit will be far more difficult if you misjudge your priorities at the beginning. In simple terms, if you don't focus on the right things first off, it will have a great impact on future results.

So, as soon as possible after starting your new job:

- Identify your own priorities
- Make self-management an unbreakable priority
- Work in such a way that you focus on your core 20 percent of key tasks

Your objective is to be seen early on to be productive and effective. Concentrate on output and results. If you're required to manage others, ensure that everyone works in a way that reflects the realities of the 80/20 rule.

ALL EYES ARE ON YOU

Your future success depends not only on yourself, but also on the people you work with, report to, or manage. If you're the boss, and others therefore have no choice but to accept you, they'll find it much easier if you're good at what you do.

What impression do you think you'll be giving to others? They'll be watching you and waiting. It won't take them long to form at least an initial view of you. You know the saying: "First impressions last."

Your boss, colleagues, and staff will:

- Observe you, your manner, and your style
- Listen to what you say and read between the lines
- Watch what you do and how you do it
- Look at the way it affects them

It's quite unnerving if you think about it too much, but there are a couple of sensible things that you can do to help you over this sticky patch. First, prepare as well as you possibly can before you start. And second, start as you mean to go on.

A GOOD BEGINNING

As you will have already realized, there are no short cuts to success as a New Kid. You can't leapfrog the process; neither can you "wing it" and make it up as you go along. If you want to make a good start, you have to make it happen. No one else can do it for you. It means hard work and self-discipline.

The advice that follows is predicated on the belief that you can be successful in your new job. You'll learn how you need to act in order to become and remain effective.

> ! Success is something that is actively gained, not achieved through good
> ● luck.

There's a saying: "Luck is a matter of preparation meeting opportunity." It's always a good idea to take advantage of any lucky opportunities that come along, but without a success strategy, luck alone will not get you where you want to be.

THE POWER OF PREPARATION

"Be prepared" is such a good motto. Once you've started your new job there may be little time for reflection. This is why in Step 1 I stressed the importance of negotiating a bit of time between jobs, if possible, to think about and prepare for your new role.

Preparation carried out correctly can:

- Secure information, allowing appropriate decisions to be made
- Make it possible to create a plan of action
- Ensure you're in a position to start as you mean to go on
- Give you confidence to proceed as you decide is right

New Kids should be able to demonstrate that they've prepared seriously. By doing this you'll make it clear to superiors, colleagues, and staff that you are well positioned to succeed. The positive effect this will have on your profile is considerable. Do your homework well and starting your new job will seem far less daunting.

ACTION PLAN

> As a New Kid, you're going to be very busy once your job gets underway, so planning and prioritizing are vital.

Your action plan could take two forms: a "self" plan and a "task" plan. Setting up an action plan will help you to remember what needs to be done, when it needs to be done by, and the impact it will have on whom and what. You could begin your self-related action plan by considering your:

- Skills
- Personality
- Knowledge (of the job, role, organization, people, product— whatever is relevant)
- Connections (who you know may be as useful as what you know)
- Profile (how you were perceived in your old organization)
- Attitudes (how they affect your work and your dealings with other people)

Match this list with your new job profile, and you'll see how you shape up. For example:
- Do you have skills that need strengthening?
- Which aspects of your personality give you an advantage?
- Which ones will you have to curb?
- Which areas of knowledge do you need to extend?
- How will you do this?
- Who do you know that might be useful to you in your new job?
- Who will you have to establish contact and develop a relationship with?

It might be sensible, when considering your answers, to take a short-term and then a long-term view. For example, it may be that some of your skills are sufficient to carry you through for the time being, while others, unless addressed immediately, will soon land you in trouble.

Once you begin your new job you'll need to prioritize the tasks ahead. Thus your task-related action plan might be to:
- Do some reading (report, brochure, file notes, new policy statement)
- Attend a course (training on a key skill or relating to your new role)
- Persuade a colleague to take a particular course of action
- Obtain briefing or permission (from your new manager) in relation to your work

If you can develop the habit of sketching out an action plan (self- or task-related) either daily, weekly, or monthly, it will be a useful aid to time management, self-organization, and effectiveness. It will be invaluable by the time you reach your appraisal date.

MORE RECONNAISSANCE
When stepping into uncharted territory, we do well to remember the old saying "Forewarned is forearmed." You'll need to ask yourself what information will be useful, and what is essential, prior to taking up your new appointment. Here are some things to consider:
- Targets (personal and group/departmental)
- Procedures and systems (What should you be familiar with ahead of time?)
- People (Who is in your team? Should you meet any of them before you start working with them? Do you know anyone who knows any of them?)

- Lines of communication and reporting (Who do you report to and who reports to you? What processes are used—meetings, written reports?)
- Controls (How do you monitor performance and progress?)
- Policy (Do you know what applies in your new situation and understand your role in it?)
- Records (What should you look at—files, notes, reports, even the contents of the stationery cupboard?)

Once you are in post, the best thing is to read everything you possibly can. It's absolutely true that information is power.

ANNOUNCING THE NEWS

By the time you start your new job, most people in the organization will hopefully have heard of your appointment. Whether you are being promoted from within or are an external appointment, it's worth checking that your name has been mentioned and that other staff know who you are and what job you are going to do.

If possible, ask your boss how colleagues and staff were told. If a note was circulated advising them of the new appointment, ask if you can see a copy. The reason for this is that further clarification may be required. Maybe a corporate email has been sent around, or perhaps a note has been posted on company notice boards. There could even be a mention in the corporate newsletter or publication. At the very least, it's essential that you should know what has been said about you in print before you start on Day One.

It's also a good idea to check which colleagues and members of staff have been told. This is not to imply that New Kids are egoists, and that nothing less than a 21-gun salute on your first day will do. (Of course, if you're taking over as chairman of the board this may be the norm.) But in practical terms it's a lot easier, and saves masses of time, if you don't have to explain the whys and wherefores of your new position to all and sundry.

PLANNING DAY ONE

The reason you need to spend some time thinking about Day One is that you don't want to spend all of your first day responding to events. It's not ideal if the people you first meet get the impression that you're unapproachable because your number-one priority at that moment is reading files.

You should consider what you are going to do on your first day. For example, if you're in charge of a number of staff, it would be sensible to convene a short staff-meeting. What sort of agenda are you going to need? You'll certainly want to get some feedback from staff on the current situation, so as to be able to organize your workload and theirs. Familiarize yourself with the office calendar system. Is it electronic? Does it show the entries for everyone in the department? If so, you should be able to figure out where the key players are at any given time.

What arrangements will you make? Are there any announcements that you should consider? How about putting a number of meetings in the calendar, and suggesting dates for discussions, decisions, deadlines, etc., both in writing and in face-to-face interviews?

It also helps to be clear from Day One about what you won't do. If you're in a position where you're responsible for junior staff, set boundaries—for example, "I will not tolerate sloppy timekeeping," or, "I'm perfectly happy to continue with the tradition of 'Happy Hour' drinks after work on Fridays."

Resolve immediately not to be railroaded into making instant decisions in response to urgent (and perhaps unreasonable) requests. "I must have a decision about my pay raise by the end of today." Why? How could you possibly deal with this, even if it's within your remit? You could not be expected to assent to or reject such an application without due consideration.

Make it clear that you've made a note of certain things that need attention, and that they will be dealt with in good time. As long as your staff feel confident that you are listening to them and are not likely to forget their requests for attention, approval, etc., you'll come across straightaway as a reasonable and fair person. What you are trying to achieve is a level playing field, so that your future dealings with them are not too problematic.

STEP 03

Here We Go: Start As You Mean To Go On

❝ Do it now, do it right, do it continually. ❞

THREE LESSONS FOR NEW KIDS EVERYWHERE

LESSON 1

A crow was sitting on a tree, doing nothing all day. A small rabbit saw the crow, and asked him, "Can I also sit like you and do nothing all day long?" The crow answered: "Sure, why not?" So, the rabbit sat on the ground below the crow, and rested. All of a sudden, a fox appeared, jumped on the rabbit, and ate it.

Message for New Kids: To be sitting and doing nothing, you must be sitting very, very high up.

LESSON 2

A turkey was chatting with a bull. "I'd love to be able to get to the top of that tree," sighed the turkey, "but I haven't got the energy." "Well, why don't you nibble on some of my droppings?" replied the bull. "They're packed with nutrients." The turkey pecked at a lump of dung and found that it actually gave him enough strength to reach the lowest branch of the tree. The next day, after eating some more dung, he reached the second branch. Finally, after a fourth night, there he was, proudly perched on the topmost branch. He was soon spotted by a farmer, who shot the turkey out of the tree.

Message for New Kids: Bullshit might get you to the top, but it won't keep you there.

LESSON 3
A little bird was flying south for the winter. It was so cold that the bird froze and fell to the ground in a large field. While it was lying there, a cow came by and dropped some dung on it. As the frozen bird lay there in a pile of cow dung, it began to realize how warm it was. The dung was actually thawing it out! It lay there all warm and happy, and soon began to sing for joy. A passing cat heard the bird singing and came to investigate. Following the sound, the cat discovered the bird under the pile of cow dung, and promptly dug it out and ate it.

Messages for New Kids:
Not everyone who shits on you is your enemy.
Not everyone who gets you out of shit is your friend.
When you're in deep shit, it's best to keep your mouth shut.

FITTING IN
You have your new job—is it going to be a dream, or a nightmare? In reality it will probably be something

between the two. So, what can you do to make sure it's nearer to the dream?

First of all, what sort of probationary period do you have? If you don't have one, perhaps it would be advisable to negotiate it. Whether it's of one month's or three months' duration, this is an important settling-in time. New Kids may think it's advantageous to the employer, but there are benefits for you too. For example, it gives both employer and New Kid an opportunity to decide whether they're getting what they want from each other.

Some points to consider:
- You may be good at the job but find you don't really like or want it
- You may not have enough (or any) autonomy
- Size does matter—do you like working for a large company? (You'll need to be good at office politics to survive.) Or would you do better in a small company, where your talents are noticed?

Sanjit, a newly appointed manager of an IT software company, advises. "In the beginning, go for plenty of interviews (even for jobs you know you don't want or can't get). This way you'll get lots of practice at answering awkward questions. Once you begin to relax, and be yourself, you won't mind the interview process at all, because it's all about confidence. Once you're confident about interviews, you'll start being offered jobs. If you're offered a job you're not sure

> about, don't be bullied into accepting it. You should play for time or have courage and walk away. The 'bird in the hand is worth two in the bush' adage may be true. But why take a job that you know won't suit you? You'll only be putting off (for a short time) the day when you hand in your notice and start the whole process all over again."

So, even when you're a New Kid, make the most of the probationary period to do your thinking. After all, you need to be sure you're in the best possible place for the next stage in your career.

> Sarah was thrilled when she landed her new job as researcher for a large technical recruitment firm. During her first week, her new boss asked if she would accompany him to a conference at which he was speaking. She jumped at the chance. They were flying from London to Edinburgh, and Sarah realized shortly after take-off that she was in for a testing time. There was a lot of turbulence and she was not good at air travel. Her boss, noticing her discomfort, turned toward her to ask if she needed a sick bag. Just at that moment, Sarah threw up all over him. She was mortified. He coped magnificently, despite being covered in vomit, and managed to arrange for a new suit to be ready for him on his arrival at his hotel, so that he was in a fit state to make his presentation.

> Despite this early setback, after a three-month probationary period, Sarah realized that the job was just what she wanted. From her boss's point of view, he was able to assess Sarah's qualities as an employee—even if any future joint trips were to be made by train!

JOINING THE "A" TEAM

Before you even begin to get down to work, consider the likely expectations of the people you'll be working with. They'll tend to define a List A colleague as one who:

- Is positive and enthusiastic
- Has vision (sees the big picture)
- Achieves their own goals
- Is well organized
- Makes good—i.e. objective—decisions
- Provides honest feedback
- Is fair and doesn't have favorites
- Is open-minded and curious
- Listens (and is available to listen)
- Knows and takes an interest in colleagues
- Is a good communicator
- Shows confidence and gives credit
- Keeps people informed
- Acknowledges their own mistakes and weaknesses
- Shares experience and helps others

Similarly, they will have firm ideas about the characteristics they dread finding in a List B colleague. This will be one who:
- Puts themselves first, always
- Fails to set clear objectives and priorities
- Is a loner (seemingly uncaring about team workers)
- Is secretive (or late in divulging information)
- Procrastinates
- Is unapproachable
- Is neither honest nor fair
- Fails to consider other people's feelings
- Allows their personal workload to prevent good team performance

Both these lists could, I'm sure, be extended. You have probably come across such people in previous jobs. But as the New Kid you'll be anxious to show most of the attributes from List A when meeting and dealing with colleagues for the first time. Let's hope you don't find many of your fellow workers demonstrating traits from List B.

> **!** Make it your business to discover what is most important to your new colleagues.

TOP TIPS FOR SURVIVING THE EARLY DAYS
- Don't give out too much information about yourself. Remember that on your first day no one will yet be feeling any loyalty toward you. Be tactful, listen, avoid

non-work gossip, smile, and remember to keep quiet and let others do the talking
- Figure out the office hierarchy by observation. It won't be as shown on the organizational chart
- Read anything and everything you can lay your hands on
- If employed as part of a team, treat the others equally, unless they all agree that one or other takes precedence. The quiet ones are often the ones who get ahead—and they might take you with them
- If you are given the opportunity to take on extra training, accept. Everything you learn is another string to your bow
- If you are asked to take on extra duties, do them—with a smile. You can, after a while, find someone "better suited" (i.e. with less work) to take them over
- Find out where the bathroom is! You don't want to get a reputation for being permanently in it—which is what might happen if you always get lost looking for it

WHERE ARE YOU COMING FROM?

At this stage in your planning and preparation, you'll need to vary your approach according to whether you are being promoted by your current employer or moving on to a new one.

CURRENT EMPLOYER

Here you'll need to keep in mind that people already know you. Your position in relation to others will—

must—change. You are moving on but staying put, if that doesn't sound too paradoxical. Because of your new role, you'll have to create a suitable "distance" between you and others. Existing relationships and friendships can't be allowed to dictate the way things will work in future. You may still be part of the same team, division, or department, in which case you'll need to give consideration to how you come across. Beware of being arrogant. Don't "throw the baby out with the bath water"—old alliances can often be useful.

NEW EMPLOYER
Bear in mind that in this case you're going to face a much steeper learning curve. Everything is going to be new. Don't act—or even give an opinion—until you have sufficient facts. Discretion and caution are the best way forward.

> ! Always match your approach to the actual circumstances and be realistic
> ● about the situation you are in.

FIRST THINGS FIRST
In order to arrive fresh and with the right mindset on your first day, start preparing the night before by organizing everything you need:
- Charge your cellphone
- Decide what you're going to wear and get it ready
- Organize your briefcase
- Make a list of "Must do's" (don't confuse this with a

"Would like to do" list, which would be much too long)
- Check your calendar for the next five days and ensure there's nothing distracting in it, such as visitors, or a dental check-up (and if there is, cancel it, so that you can focus on your work without interruption)
- Review transportation arrangements—is there enough gas in your car, is your train or bus ticket valid?
- Check your travel route for any unexpected problems—roadworks, train cancellations, strikes, etc.
- Set your alarm and allow yourself at least 30 minutes' extra time to get to work
- Go to bed early and get some sleep

And just for the record, if you don't want to succeed on your first day, here are some of the mistakes made by new employees that ensured they lost their jobs quite quickly:
- Arriving anything up to an hour late on their first day, or turning up on the wrong day
- Offering excuses for bad timekeeping, such as falling asleep on the train and missing the station
- Not being able to find their smart shoes
- Going to the wrong building
- Getting out of the elevator on the wrong floor
- Wearing inappropriate clothing (a transparent blouse or inappropriately short skirt for women, a T-shirt with an inappropriate slogan or ill-fitting/ripped jeans for men)

- Calming their nerves beforehand with a gin and tonic (or two)
- Being so scared that they bring their mom along with them

DAY ONE AS THE NEW KID ON THE BLOCK

What is expected of you as New Kid in terms of start and finish times? Is it OK to start at 9 a.m. and finish at 6 p.m., or are there unwritten rules about getting in before 8 a.m.? Similarly with lunch hours, New Kids need to find out whether taking time out to go shopping or visit the gym is acceptable. Or is the view that you should work at your desk through lunch?

> Ben recently joined a global telecom company as UK Marketing Director. It was corporate policy for all directors to start work at 7 a.m. (at the latest). As New Kid director he was expected to attend meetings at 6.30 or 7 a.m.—which proved difficult, as the first train didn't arrive until 7.45. So he had to drive to the office. However, he made every effort not to stay late in the evening.
>
> This "macho" approach to work was reflected in thecomposition of the board and senior management— there were very few women. The only solution was to try to play the game (if you can't beat 'em, join 'em). He stood tall and showed his strength

> (as New Kid on the Block) and came across as someone who could get things done without having to live in the office.

There will be so much to get your head around when moving into a new situation. Most important:

- **Try to get to see your boss early on.** Confirm your role and priorities and set up the communications procedure between you. Be sure of the main messages you want to get across and ask appropriate questions. Ideally, these should show your knowledge and intellect. The purpose of this meeting is to help both of you make the first few days go smoothly. Showing a positive attitude will go down well
- **Arrange introductions to other key people.** If your work involves contacts with others (another department, people on the same level as you, etc.), make sure you know them and begin to cultivate a relationship from the word go. Do your research and come across as being well informed about the people you are meeting and the part of the organization they represent. This will flatter them and show that you are committed and serious
- **Meet your own team/colleagues/staff.** As soon as you get the opportunity, ask them questions. People are generally more engaged when they're talking and being listened to than the other way around. Find out at the outset what issues are important to them and what they would most like to get out of working with you

> **!** Be enthusiastic—smile. It's infectious and hard to resist. The person you are replacing may not have been upbeat and energetic. If you show you're keen, it's sure to encourage all your colleagues to support you while you're the New Kid.

It may be a cliché, but bear in mind that you only get one chance to make a good first impression. And you can remember how to make such an impression by learning the mnemonic **I M P A C T**:

- Instigate social activities outside of work
- Manage your time effectively
- Present yourself well
- Ask questions
- Contribute ideas
- Think before you speak

Checklist for Day One:
- Be sure to arrive on time (or even a bit early)
- Look the part (think about what you wear)
- Make a point of speaking to everyone
- If this isn't possible (someone may be off sick or on vacation), set a time for an initial word
- Introduce yourself, giving some information that people will remember, for example:
  "This is my very first job and I'll probably ask lots of questions, but that's because I'm really keen to learn."

"Until last week I was living on an island in the Outer Hebrides, so not only am I coping with a new office, but I'm finding the rush hour a bit of a challenge."

- Answer any immediate questions
- Begin to show yourself as the person you want to be
- Ask questions and canvass opinion from colleagues as to how they view your input and what will be most helpful to the team

Remember to keep initial exchanges simple but positive. Don't be afraid to put things on ice for a while if you're unsure. Be honest. ("I can't answer that now. Give me a day or two to find out and I'll come back to you.") Keep notes—and keep promises made during such conversations.

If something can go wrong in the first few days in your new job, it probably will! You park in the boss's parking space. You make your coffee in someone's special cup. You jam the photocopier when photocopying something personal . . .

Mike was eager to get home after his first day in his new job as project supervisor. The office was emptying as staff were preparing to leave. He said goodbye to his new colleagues, grabbed the briefcase next to his desk, and left for the station. On opening the case on the train home he realized that, though identical in style, it was not his own. Checking the contents, Mike discovered a selection of erotic reading materials and other interesting accessories! He decided discretion was the best course, locked the case in his car trunk, told his partner a white lie about having accidentally left his bag at the office, and got to the office extra early the next morning so that he could replace the bag without being seen. Mike never discovered who the case belonged to.

SIZING THINGS UP

You'll need to begin to get the measure of people early on. To be successful at this, New Kids don't need to be expert psychologists, but it might help!

For the rest, here are a few tips:
- Listen to what people say and how they say it
- Read between the lines
- Check immediately anything that is unclear
- Address (or note) any apparent hidden agendas
- Be aware of informal communications channels as well as the official ones
- Note any areas requiring further investigation

You need to get to know your colleagues, how they work, their strengths and weaknesses. This can't be done in five minutes. As mentioned in Step 2, while tasks might be accomplished quickly, people-related activities take longer.

It's an essential process that should be started early and handled sensitively.

If properly managed, working relationships can be extremely rewarding. The trick for New Kids is to recognize the big psychological challenge they face and not to shy away from it. Awareness is the key. Some people are particularly nervous of change. They may be shy, insecure, feel threatened by newcomers, or somewhat envious of your success. Keep an eye on your specific duties; look carefully around you to see how your work interacts with others'. If there are things you'd like to change, make a note of them for the future. Also observe things that are non-negotiable.

People who have been in post much longer than you will want to feel that little bit in control, no matter how senior to them you are. In the early days, observation and information-gathering are crucial. Watch how people work. Ask them how they like their colleagues to work. For example, will they mind you popping into their office (or work area) if you need to discuss something? Or would they prefer a slightly more formal approach—a regular daily meeting or an email request?

You could even go as far as asking your team workers what they would list as the ten most important skills for your job. It's certainly one way of finding out what their priorities are, and what makes them tick.

Don't be too worried if you find one or two colleagues extremely difficult in the first few encounters. They're probably just trying to make their mark. There's every likelihood that once they're more used to you, they'll feel less threatened and will calm down.

The reason that establishing good working relationships takes time is that you're trying to develop trust, earn respect, and build up confidence. This is a two-way process. You may be more adept than some of your colleagues at establishing a smooth working relationship. But persevere. Once they know that, despite being the New Kid, you are "on their side," the ogres who seemed to appear on all sides on your first day may turn into allies and even friends in the months to come.

Avoid making and acting on unwarranted assumptions about people early on. Suspend reaction in order to avoid being judgmental.

YOUR FIRST MEETING

It may not be possible to arrange this on your first day, but your boss will soon want to introduce you, the New Kid, formally. If you are the boss yourself, it will be up to you to arrange the meeting, and you should try to do it early on. Meetings speak volumes about people, so make sure your meeting etiquette is polished.

Here's a plan for your initial meeting:
- Set a time and date that is convenient to as many people as possible (you may be able to check this yourself with the office calendar, or get some help from staff or co-workers)

- Make all necessary practical arrangements (venue, refreshments, avoidance of interruption through call divert, booking a separate meeting room, etc.)
- Issue a concise agenda in advance
- Make sure the agenda is appropriate, fits the time available, and is of relevance to all those attending
- Make it clear to those who will be speaking what you expect from them (e.g. are they to give a visual presentation?)
- Set start and finish times for others' contributions—and try to stick to them (you are setting an example here, so be sure to start the meeting on time too)
- Give everyone the chance to have a say—listen, make notes, and be seen to take an interest in their views
- Make any action points clear (for the group or for individuals)
- Link to the next meeting (for which you might set a date)
- Confirm any follow-up actions in writing

The purpose of a meeting is to motivate people and precipitate actions. People will be wondering how your presence and style will affect them. By conducting a good meeting, show them that your influence in the department/team/group is going to be a positive one.

SETTING THE AGENDA

The agenda for such a meeting will depend on your precise role. It's likely that it will include such items as:

- Your understanding of the role of the team and its immediate goals
- Any necessary explanations regarding your appointment (e.g. why you've been brought in or promoted to group leader)
- The current position (how things are going, what problems have occurred, what opportunities are available)
- A chance to ask questions
- Details of, and reasons for, any important changes in working practices
- Procedures regarding reporting and communications (e.g. when and how you plan to keep in touch with both individuals and the group)
- Action points on urgent operational issues

Remember to ask as much as tell, and listen to the answers. Avoid change for its own sake. If changes are necessary, give good reasons, preferably backed up by facts. However logical changes may be, people will be suspicious. They will naturally be wary— you're a New Kid, after all. Isn't that what New Kids all do? Immediately set about introducing new procedures and systems? Their overriding thought will be, "How will these changes affect me and my position within the group/department/organization?"

So, take the time and trouble to explain things from their point of view. When you're a New Kid, empathy is your greatest ally in dealing with colleagues, team workers, and staff.

EARLY ACTIONS

Here is something every New Kid should do as early on as possible— though you must act only on the basis of firm information:

- Identify an issue that is seen as requiring attention
- Sort it out

If possible, you should be able to:

- Tell people that you see this issue as a priority, something that can't be left unaddressed
- Explain the basis of your decision
- Specify the action to be taken (this could be a temporary measure)
- Take any additional action necessary (confirm in writing, consult with a colleague outside of your section)
- Get it off the department's "To do" list promptly and definitely

What you are looking for here is an issue that is generally considered to be due (or overdue) for attention. It will be seen that it is now being resolved, which establishes you, the New Kid, as someone prepared to take action. Select your item carefully, act in a considered fashion, and clear the deck of one outstanding issue. This not only helps the whole department/organization, but it also speaks volumes, in a positive way, about you too.

GROUND RULES

Before we go any further, remember that as a New Kid you must observe certain ground rules. Successful integration into the new workplace requires some consultation. Things work best when there's no argument. If too much lengthy consultation is involved, time runs out, things don't get done, and everyone is worse off. Some things must work by diktat.

Such things include dress code, what can be claimed on expenses, flexibility over working hours, vacation entitlement, etc. In such matters people are expected to toe the line. There should be no time wasted on arguments about "exceptions." Find out as early on as possible what the office dos and don'ts are. If there's a workplace manual on the intranet, make sure you refer to it. It could be that the HR director will issue you with guidance regarding such rules. If in doubt, ask. Rules, such as whether or not you're expected to attend all departmental meetings, are important. It wouldn't look good as New Kid if you failed to appear at your first meeting simply because you hadn't been told of the location or time.

> ! How you act in your first few days affects your profile within the company.

> ❝The man who has confidence in himself gains the confidence of others.❞
>
> *Hasidic Saying*

STEP 04

A Matter Of Timing:
The Importance Of Getting And Keeping Yourself Organized

> ❝ Tomorrow is always the busiest day of the week. ❞
>
> *Jonathan lazair*

New Kids are a bit like mountaineers attempting to scale the north face of the Eiger. You need to be fit, prepared, and organized. Whatever your new job is, you'll be expected to achieve particular things. To achieve anything you have to be organized, and in the hectic first few days in your new job you'll need to be exceptionally well prepared. If you're a New Kid manager, you'll need to make sure that your staff are well organized too. There's nothing better than leading by example.

If you can do anything to give yourself a head start in the first few hours, or days, you should do so. No New Kid wants to give the impression of being a headless chicken, led by events rather than being in control.

As a New Kid, it's crucial to keep your eyes above the desk and spend time absorbing as much information as you possibly can about company policies, procedures, systems, and routines. You'll never be able to remember everything, so you need some effective recording system that will save you precious time now and prevent crises and problems arising in future. How about a notebook?

You may be the sort of New Kid who is brought into an organization to make changes, ensure progress is maintained, or develop a new project or system. You don't want to spend all your time fire fighting, so get yourself in shape from Day One.

TIME MANAGEMENT

Does managing your time really matter? Is it important? For New Kids, the answer is emphatically—yes! Without an ability to manage time, in those precious first few days and weeks you'll achieve less and have minimal productivity.

Your time should and must be managed. Controlling time means coping better with the elements of surprise that erode everyone's working day, and this applies in particular to New Kids.

If steps are taken to avoid interruptions, productivity and achievement immediately rise. There's no magic formula here. To a degree, success lies in the details and the effect is cumulative: everything you do, every constructive habit you develop, can help improve your situation.

Mark Forster, author of *Get Everything Done and Still Have Time To Play*, says, "You can't manage your time well unless you know what you want to achieve." But in order to do that, it helps to know *yourself*.

Do you know what makes you tick in the workplace? Some people function effectively late into the evening yet can't cope with a dawn start. It would be a bit of a shock for a New Kid if you were used to getting into the office around 9.30 a.m. and found that in your new job departmental staff-briefings always started at 8 a.m. on a Monday morning.

What type of New Kid are you? When are the peaks and troughs of your day?

THE EARLY RISER

Some people wake up at 7.00 a.m. (or even earlier) raring to go. If you're not a New Kid dawn starter, avoid arranging breakfast meetings! You'll need a slightly later start in order to be effective. One thing that does help is bright sunny mornings. Waking up to sunlight is a natural alarm call, and the more you can soak up, the livelier you'll feel.

RELUCTANT RISERS

If you're a New Kid who finds early mornings difficult, you really should find time for breakfast. It needs to be simple but nutritious. Cereals such as bran flakes and oats are high in fiber and slow energy-releasers, and if taken with some fruit will help to maintain your blood-sugar levels (and also your energy levels) throughout the day.

TRAVELERS

On the way to work, New Kids should not simply doze—particularly if they're driving a car! If there's some background reading to be done, a train or bus journey is an excellent time to do it. Filler tasks, such as drafting, writing lists, or skimming through professional journals, are ideal.

PLANNERS

New Kids who like making lists should start with a daily task-sheet. Make a list numbered from 1 to 10, or rank your tasks like celebrities—A or B List. Isolate the three most important tasks and make sure you complete them on your first day. Ticking them off once they've been fully completed will give you a great sense of satisfaction. New Kids need to feel that they've achieved something and this is an excellent way of making a start.

BRAINY TYPES

Are you a New Kid egghead? When do you have your blinding ideas and brainpower surges? Whenever or wherever it is, make sure you have your notebook with you in which to record your thoughts. You may not always be at your desk when this happens. Research has shown that women are likely to have their most creative thoughts when talking to friends and men when in the bathroom!

LUNCHERS

Some New Kids find the break in the working day regenerating. But it is sensible to avoid huge meals. If possible, choose a light lunch or a healthy snack and take some exercise to avoid the afternoon slump. Walking and breathing deeply help you to stay alert till the end of the day.

P.M. BLUES

To avoid this energy low-point, New Kids should make sure their posture is correct and have regular drinks of water. If you're in the middle of a long and tedious piece of work, do some exercises at your desk to pep up your metabolism. You could take a walk around the office and make the most of the opportunity to engage in conversation and information-gathering. Caffeine breaks can be extremely useful.

LATE TASKERS

At the end of the day, New Kids should get into the habit of making the next day's work easier by writing a new "To do" list. Begin by listing the tasks you'll tackle first thing in the morning. If you've made a decision to take regular exercise, then start as you mean to go on and fit in a workout at the gym, or find time for a swim. Alternatively, take a brisk walk home and avoid the crowded buses and trains.

GETTING ORGANIZED

> ! It's not the hours you work that are important, but what you do during those hours.

It's often reported that workers would like to reduce or at least control the amount of time they spend working. If you as a New Kid are going to succeed in being productive—certainly if you are to achieve a satisfactory work/life balance—you need to monitor your new situation from the start.

Questions for New Kids: in your last job, did you:
- Regularly spend more than ten hours a day working?

- Need to take work home three or more times a week?
- Find yourself dreaming about your job?
- Have sleepless nights because of work pressures?
- Cancel vacation or weekend plans because of work pressures?

If you have answered yes to three or more of the above, you certainly don't want to repeat the pattern in this new job. New Kids, here's how to improve the situation.

> **!** The key is being able to achieve results *without* working hopelessly long hours. If you are seen to be effective, particularly in these crucial early days, then you'll be regarded as efficient.

Because you're in a new situation, it's important to keep an eye on the organizational culture:
- Become aware of the rules of the workplace—fast
- Is a tidy desk seen as a sign of an efficient person?
- Or is an empty in-tray seen as a sign of an empty mind?
- Does the company have a "presenteeism" culture?
- Is it wise to be seen leaving your workplace on time every day?

New Kids should make every effort to support the ethos of the company from day one. If you've been brought in as a "new broom," your ability to manage change and add value is imperative, but your approach should not run counter

to the company's policy or corporate identity. For example:
- Create a reputation for adding value by improving the performance/morale of your group/department
- Learn how to manage change positively and productively to achieve good results

Your time should be organized in such a way that you're focused right away on what is most important. Everything about your New Kid approach must assist in promoting good productivity. Again, there are many ways to do this, including the following:
- Spend time on planning and thinking (for the day/week/month ahead)
- If you spend time prioritizing your week, you need only spend a few minutes prioritizing your day
- Make sure you know what is urgent and deal with it first (and if in doubt, ask—you'll be glad you did)

You could, as New Kid, get down to some serious chunking—and unfortunately that doesn't mean getting stuck into a triple burger or a huge bar of chocolate!

New Kids—get your tasks sorted:
- Print out emails, dig out letters and faxes—list them all
- Sort them into piles relating to the task required—write/meet/ call/delegate
- Set aside some time each day for interacting with staff and colleagues—but do set a limit and stick to it
- Actively delegate tasks and responsibilities to members

of your department (where appropriate)
- Set achievable deadlines for them
- Aim to complete three of the tasks on your daily task-list
- Plan some time out for relaxation—take a break and stand back from your work for a few minutes, chat to a colleague, or go for a walk around the block

What makes all this possible for New Kids? The answer is simple—it's you. You must create your own destiny, fast, in terms of time and productivity.

> **!** It helps to think things through, focus on individualelements, and categorize your tasks in some way.

There are four key areas that will take up a lot of a New Kid's time:
- Routine communications: paperwork, admin, exchanging information
- Traditional role: planning, controlling, decision making (for yourself if you don't have responsibility for others)
- People management: motivation, conflict resolution, discipline, training, development
- Networking: essential for New Kids who need to enhance their profile by interacting with others both within and outside of the company

With this sort of manageable picture in mind, as New Kid you should find it easier to take concrete steps to organize yourself. How exactly, you may ask? You need a New Kid action plan.

ORGANIZATIONAL ACTION PLAN

Decide how much time you're going to devote to each of the above categories each day/week in order to create your own time-management activity sheet. Block out the time, set against it the appropriate task, and estimate the amount of time required. This should be incorporated into your daily planner and, if appropriate, the departmental electronic calendar.

Ideally, the day should be divided into chunks to reflect the various demands of the role. (For the purposes of this illustration, we have labeled the four types of New Kid tasks A, B, C, and D. This does not reflect their order of priority.)

Routine communications	A tasks
Traditional role	B tasks
People management	C tasks
Networking	D tasks

New Kid Time/Activity Sheet		
Day: .... Week commencing:		
Before 9 a.m.	A tasks	(paperwork)
	D tasks	(networking breakfasts)
9 a.m.	C tasks	(staff meetings)
10 a.m.	B tasks	(planning, decision making)
11 a.m.	B tasks	(planning, decision making)
12 p.m.	D tasks	(reception)
1 p.m.	D tasks	(client lunch meeting)
2 p.m.	C tasks	(staff interviews/appraisal)
3 p.m.	A tasks	(admin/exchange information)
4 p.m.	B tasks	(planning)
5 p.m.	A tasks	(paperwork)
6 p.m. and after	D tasks	(presentations)

Example:

New Kid Time/Activity Sheet		
Day: Tuesday	Week commencing: November 7th	
07.00	A tasks	train to Bristol (reading/timesheets)
07.45	D tasks	Chamber of Commerce business breakfast
09.15	C tasks	return train journey (reading/write report)
10.00	B tasks	departmental meeting (staff appraisals)
11.30	B tasks	desk work (forecast for 2006)
12.00	D tasks	Partners' meeting (pre-lunch reception)
12.45	D tasks	Williams Seymour (client lunch)
14.30	C tasks	interview (assistant manager replacement)
15.30	A tasks	PA (delegation of weekly admin)
16.00	B tasks	presentation for client meeting (final check)
17.30	A tasks	preparation for Wednesday
18.30–20.00	D tasks	South West regional presentation

SMART PLANNING

New Kids will need to plan the work and work the plan. You not only need a plan; you need to develop a method for **S M A R T** working:

- **Set task times:** Divide your day/week into sections. If you want to be at your desk on Mondays, avoid meetings that take you out of your office. If you like to catch up with end-of-week tasks on Fridays, block out the time to do this
- **Make goals:** Clearly defined objectives help to focus the mind and keep you motivated. Avoid setting yourself unachievable deadlines
- **Ask for help:** Never muddle through. Delegate anything you can. Enlist the expertise of others whose skills complement your own
- **Reflect rather than react:** Avoid committing to anything until you have all the facts—a hasty decision could lead to unnecessary stress
- **Think—use your brain:** Never be afraid to leave a task if you're stumped. As in an exam, if you switch to another task rather than dwelling on the problem, by the time you return to it your subconscious may well have produced a solution

STAYING "ON PLAN"

Patrick Forsyth, a highly respected writer and trainer in management techniques, is author of *Detox Your Career* and *Manage Your Boss*. His advice on organization for New Kids is to keep to a time-management plan.

There are three main factors that combine to keep New Kids from completing planned tasks. These are:
- Other people
- Events
- You

Let's start with you. You may put off a task because you:
- Are unsure of what to do
- Dislike the task
- Prefer to do a different task (despite the clear priority of this one)
- Fear the consequences

(New Kids, don't worry. There are people who have ticked all four of these reasons.)

Time can also be wasted in the reverse way. What tasks do you spend too long on (or resist delegating) because you like them? Be honest.

Overdoing things is often a major cause of wasted time, as is flattering yourself that no one else can do a particular task as well as you can. This is a mistake no New Kid can afford to make, because in the early days of your new job, every second counts.

As a New Kid, you may be reluctant to delegate to someone else in case they prove to be more adept at the task than you. This is worth giving some thought to. It may just be a one-off, the result of being in a new post. But if this is an area that could develop, there's huge potential for wasting time on a regular basis.

New Kids, note: there are certain time-management rules that are important. One is the fallacy that things get easier if left. The reverse is almost always true. Faced with firing a member of staff, to take a dramatic example, a New Kid manager might constantly prevaricate. You may feel you want to "see how things go," "check the end-of-month results," etc., when swift action (all the necessary checks in fact having been made) is best all around.

Other people can also conspire to keep New Kids from their key tasks. You'll soon find that when certain colleagues stick their heads around the door and say, "Hi, have you got a minute?" half an hour minimum is about to vanish unconstructively. Saying no as a New Kid is not that easy. You don't want to seem brusque or unfriendly. But being firm about unwanted visitors is an inherent part of good time management.

Telephones can be the bane of New Kids' lives. Voicemail in all its various forms is supposed to save hours of time, but it can also reduce the chances of relationship building if used excessively. New Kids should use voicemail with caution. It's all too easy for colleagues to say, "It's no use calling him—his phone is always switched to voicemail." This is a negative viewpoint and one that all New Kids should be at pains to avoid.

There are moments when it's good to be unavailable. Some tasks can be completed in a quiet hour yet take much longer if you are constantly interrupted. New Kids, you'll find that, at the beginning, tasks take longer anyway, simply because you're doing everything for the first time.

If you're engaged in a task that requires some real thought or creativity, try to do it in an interruption-free zone.

> **!** When you start your new job and are inputting numbers into your phone—cellphone or other—key in for each contact "(w)" (work), "(o)" (office), "(h)" (home), or "(c)" (cellphone), so that you don't have to waste time looking them up. It saves hours . . .

There are a number of ways in which New Kids can avoid interruptions to a planned schedule:
- Limit the number of times you check email—perhaps to twice a day
- Make use of cancellations by having some filler tasks ready
- Ensure that meetings have a short agenda and set a time limit
- If you work in an office that has a door, close it at certain times: this will stop casual interruptions (only those with important queries will try to gain entry, and, as a New Kid, you'll be making a statement)

PRIORITIZING

> ! You must prioritize. If you know
> what your priorities areand organize
> ● accordingly, you'll achieve more. It
> helpsas a New Kid if you do one thing at
> a time.

The ability to prioritize is essential.

> One chief executive had to decide which were the most important tasks for him to tackle. Each day he made a list of the things he wanted to get done. He divided his list into categories A and B. He tore the list in half. He put the B List into the waste bin and kept the A List. He then divided the A List into A and B categories and repeated the process. After three attempts he arrived at the matters most urgently requiring his attention and dealt with them straightaway. This might not suit everyone (though do try it!), but you do need to approach things in a systematic way.

Effective prioritizing is what all New Kids need to be able to do. You should also develop the habit of doing things you don't like and getting them out of the way. If you can distinguish the important from the unimportant, you'll instantly feel more in control and your work will be more efficient. Important tasks require quality time.

Urgent tasks have to be done quickly, otherwise problems will arise.

Here's the classic diagram with quadrants showing the four basic categories for defining tasks (you've probably seen it before—but it still works):

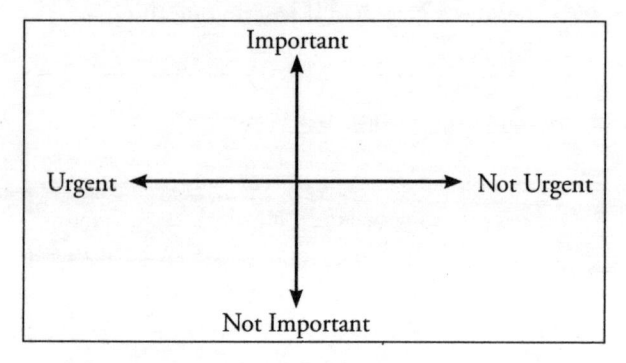

```
                    Important
                        ↑
                        |
    Urgent  ←———————————+———————————→  Not Urgent
                        |
                        ↓
                  Not Important
```

Assign each of your tasks to one or more of the quadrants, as appropriate. Then:
- If a task is both urgent and important, put it at the top of your A List
- Deal with the urgent tasks first, but deal with them quickly (these are the fire-fighting, crisis-management tasks)
- Spend as much time as possible on tasks that are important but not urgent (these are the things that will have the most impact on your new role)
- For New Kids, most tasks that are neither important nor urgent are best outsourced or ignored—you simply must concentrate on what needs to be done

Rules for the well-organized New Kid:
- Make the most of your personal strengths
- Make full use of technology—where appropriate, let the machines take the strain
- Be punctual and use time gaps for filler tasks
- Take regular breaks—schedule coffee, lunch, and tea breaks so as to maximize relationship building in non-prime working time
- Keep your desk/work area clear of junk

> A young assistant, at an early stage in his career, was asked by his senior manager to attend a meeting that was being held in Conference Room C at 9.30 a.m. When he arrived he found that the door was locked. He tried to enter, but could not gain admittance. He asked several people whether the meeting had been relocated, but no one knew anything about it. Some time later he saw his boss and explained that he'd been unable to attend the meeting as he hadn't been able to discover where it was being held. He was told that it had taken place in Conference Room C at 9.30 a.m. The young man assured the manager that he had tried to get in. His manager explained that the procedure in his department was to lock the door at the designated starting time. The assistant was never late again.
> *(true story recounted by Patrick Forsyth)*

With regard to time management and personal organization, New Kids can be effective right from the word go. You need to be strict with yourself and with others. It may seem difficult at first, but if you can get to grips with it, your workload will seem much less daunting.

NEW KIDS AND WORKAHOLISM

Isn't it easy to say at the start of a new job, "I'll stay late and do this," or "I'll come in early," or "I'll work on it over the weekend"?

Being busy is not the same as being effective. And being over-busy, and either liking it or persuading yourself that there's no other way, defines being a workaholic. New Kids, this is harmful to everyone, but particularly to yourself. If you start your new job by working an 18-hour day, when everyone else works an average of eight hours, it can become an addiction and lead to a vicious circle where, New Kid workaholic,

- You find it impossible to say no
- "Mission Impossible"—yes, that's for me
- You actively avoid accepting offers of help
- You simply can't (or won't) delegate for fear that the job will be less well done
- You develop a reputation for getting things done to the extent that even more work is heaped on you

If you think there's even a chance of a situation like this developing, turn to the section on assertive behavior in Step 8 and read it at once!

Don't allow your new job to get you stressed in the early days. New Kids should bear the following tips in mind:

- Laughter is a great leveler—retain your sense of humor
- If something has gone wrong, don't take it personally—leave it and move on
- Be flexible—the best-laid plans don't always work out
- If the going gets tough—go shopping . . .
- Focus on a treat—the weekend is only a few days away

> Good time management is an asset to your early productivity and effectiveness. If you can develop good habits now, you'll save yourself hours of effort and energy.

ORGANIZING INFORMATION

When it comes to your database, cleanliness is definitely next to godliness.

If your contacts are moth-eaten, out of date, and choked by dead wood, there's no way you'll be able to optimize their worth. Add new and potentially exciting contacts, and they'll be swamped by the old material and sink without trace within a short space of time.

The information you record on your business connections should include:

- Your contact's name, address, telephone number, fax, and email
- Their company name and job title
- Details of first meeting (venue, who introduced you)
- What transpired

- What type of person they seemed to be (cold, tepid, or warm)
- What arrangements were made for follow-up (method, timing)
- Personal details (birthday, family, hobbies/interests)
- Geographical details (area of country, if visiting)
- Background (personal, company, previous positions held)
- Aims and objectives
- Links and mutual acquaintances

Spending some time on a database cleanse and update not only refreshes your memory as to what's in it, but helps you figure out which contacts will connect well with your new acquaintances. From here you can begin to create even more exciting and harmonious relationships, which you can develop with your newly acquired skills.

Step 05

Listen Carefully, I Shall Say This Only Once: The Importance Of Clear Communication

> **❝**Nothing astonishes men so much as common sense and plain dealing.**❞**
>
> *Ralph Waldo Emerson*

One of the things that is most likely to make a bad impression on your colleagues and staff when you're a New Kid is being a poor communicator. They would define this as giving information that is:

- Unclear
- Ambiguous
- Insufficient
- Too late (kept to yourself for too long)
- Irrelevant (not relating to their point of view)

When starting a new job, it's vital to communicate well with your new boss, colleagues, and staff. To do so you should:

- Use appropriate methods (meeting, memo, email, text message, notice board)
- Choose the right perspective (talk about "we" rather than "I," and put things personally—"you'll find" rather than "this is the case")

- Use good communication principles (keep it simple, make it clear, be precise and succinct)
- Explain both the "what" and the "why"

Communicating is one of the most important aspects of your work. New Kids keen to make the right impression should ensure that their expertise in this area is good. If you feel the need to refresh your skills, do so. Don't be afraid to ask. Ignoring failings or uncertainties risks disaster sooner or later.

As a New Kid your communications will be looked at, listened to, and carefully scrutinized. Lines will be read between, and inferences about you and about the way you do things will be drawn—for good or ill.

While considering your communication skills, make one firm rule for yourself: Always be courteous to your colleagues and staff.

That old saying is very valid: courtesy costs nothing. Any temptation that staff may offer to descend into insulting language should be resisted, as to do so could cause problems (as could even being offhand toward them). It will certainly not engender respect. This applies across the board, whatever the provocation.

If you think you're in danger of erupting in these first few tense and stressful days, remember to keep cool, count to ten (or more if necessary), and moderate your language and your manner.

The most important point about communication is that you need to be constantly well informed about what's going on. This is vital in the early days as a New Kid. If you don't know what's going on in your department or section, or in the organization as a whole, how can you possibly do your job and be seen to be effective?

THE GRAPEVINE

It's essential that you pay as much attention to informal communications as to formal ones. The need for a good network of contacts is key. This is not easy in the early days, as it takes time to establish. But if you can tap in to the grapevine (and they exist in every organization) it will help.

Infiltrating this informal communication channel requires some specific actions:

- Discover how it works and who is pivotal to its operation
- Get yourself "plugged in"
- Remember that communication is two-way (you must contribute to receive)
- Use it constructively—ignore and do not start rumors
- Use it for firm information, early warning, and dissemination
- Keep your eyes and ears open

WHY DO WE NEED TO COMMUNICATE?

At its core—and this is particularly important for all New Kids— communication is about relating to other people. Because you're just starting your new job, particularly if you're in management or a supervisory position, you'll spend about half your time generating or receiving information.

The remainder will be spent using that information or passing it on to someone else. In one form or another you are disseminating information by either absorbing it or dispensing it.

Communicating is something everyone does, but in the context of business it's more than just exchanging information. First you receive it and then you transmit it to someone else in the organization. For New Kids potential problems can accumulate in the first few days, creating confusion or even chaos. Maximizing the effectiveness of communication takes time. But it's time well spent.

For example, if a swift decision can be taken to avert a problem, it needs to be made and communicated quickly and clearly to all staff. If it's a more complex rather than an urgent issue, it may require consideration, consultation, and planning. By spending time getting communications right, effective New Kids ensure better performance from their team and show commitment to the communication process.

Communication is closely aligned with motivation. If part of your new role is to motivate people, you have to be creative, not reactive. Creating communication opportunities requires "going the extra mile." Being a New Kid, you're likely to introduce a new process in your department or sector at some stage, if not immediately. This will no doubt require staff training. Why not organize a get-together afterward?

If you do this, it will both reinforce the impression that you know that people matter and provide valuable feedback on whether the training was adequate and well received. It will also act as an indicator as to how successful the implementation of the new process is likely to be. Does everyone now understand how it works? For a New Kid, this information is important.

Whatever the issue, whether it's a new initiative or a routine situation, New Kids should understand that communication is about getting results. It requires relating to other people and getting your message across. Don't allow poor communication methods to dilute the effectiveness of your performance in the first few weeks of your new job.

> **!** Work at your corporate communication skills so that you can gain every
> **●** possible type of advantage from giving clear messages.

ARE YOU RECEIVING ME?

Communication in the workplace is a broad concept. How you, as a New Kid, interpret it depends on your organization, its culture, and its staff. Where there's a culture in the organization that is supportive of good staff communication, it will be appreciated up and down the hierarchy. In the first few days in your new job, make it one of your priorities to become familiar with the communication culture.

New Kids should have a creative approach to communication. Handled correctly, it will help to get you noticed. You can influence the company culture, but you shouldn't try to dominate it. New Kid managers have a responsibility to influence the culture and you should actively work to create one that is helpful and holistic.

If the lead in establishing the communication culture in an organization comes from the top, this is beneficial, but you shouldn't despair if it does not. As a New Kid you have the perfect opportunity to take the initiative in creating and maintaining a culture and encouraging other colleagues to play their part.

Communicating at work covers everything from conducting interviews, staff appraisal, motivation, working in teams, and all types of business processes, operations, and reviews through to holding meetings and how the computers network. It's a lot for New Kids to assimilate when there's so much else for them to come to terms with.

The process can be usefully divided into three broad areas:

- Communicating face to face
- Dealing with technology
- The interpersonal areas of relationship building, such as dealing with difficulties and feedback

You probably got a lot of experience in communicating in your previous jobs, and already know a good deal about it. Can you think of one or two good communicators you've worked with? Who have you met recently who excelled in communication skills? What particularly impressed you about them? What was it that they did so well? Try to emulate them in some way. It will give you confidence when dealing with new situations if you can recall that a particular approach worked successfully in the past.

Conversely, you've probably been in situations where someone was communicating badly. What did they do that particularly struck you? What was it that made you aware that their chosen method wasn't working? How did you feel about it?

When you're a New Kid, people won't know that some of the ideas you come up with are not yours or are not new. It's sensible to fall back on past experience and methods that have been shown to work. Of course, one of the taboos is to preface every remark with, "This is how we did it at my old job." That will produce negative results.

To put communication in the workplace in context, your New Kid antennae need to be functioning well. You need to be aware of what's happening around you. Observe the way other colleagues communicate. Note when communication does and doesn't work.

As an exercise, think about three episodes in your previous job where communication was the focus. They could be a discussion, a meeting, a phone call, exchanging an email, or reading a report or a letter. Review these situations in your mind and see if you can recall:

- The person with whom you were communicating
- The purpose of the communication
- The means by which it took place
- The outcome

Did things go as you expected in each case?

When it comes to your own communication skills, do you generally get the result you expect? Do you get a pleasant outcome more often than not? What happens when things don't turn out exactly as you'd anticipated?

Good New Kid communicators know how to command attention. If you don't get attention, how can you come across effectively and make an impact? Of course, not every method of gaining attention is desirable: shouting, wearing inappropriate clothing, and bad behavior will all get you attention, sure enough, but it won't be the right sort.

In order to create an impact, New Kids are looking to get a positive result from communicating with others in as short a time as possible. So, what type of communication method will you choose that will best express the message you want to convey?

- Is an informal chat the best approach?
- Would a meeting work better?
- What would a formal presentation achieve?
- How about a written report to the board?
- Should you put an announcement on the website?

The channel of communication you choose can greatly influence the likelihood of getting your message across.

Being a New Kid, you may unknowingly choose the wrong channel of communication and then wonder why it has failed in its purpose. There's nothing worse than relying on an impersonal approach (email, written instruction, using another member of staff as messenger) when what's really needed is one-to-one contact.

GROUP COMMUNICATION

With group communication, New Kids should remember that the message needs to come across clearly to each and every person in the group. To be an effective group communicator a New Kid needs to understand how the members of the group are linked. This requires some fairly swift action on your part. You'll need to find out how these people are interrelated, so that you can get involved in these relationships and ensure that they remain strong and continue to flourish.

For example, one of your initiatives as New Kid could involve bringing a fresh group of people together. You should begin by making sure that they all understand why they're there. This is referred to as the **forming** process:

- What is the purpose of the group?
- What is holding them together?
- What are they prepared, and not prepared, to do?
- What rules are there for working together?
- How will those outside of the group respond to them?
- What is the best outcome (and the worst) likely to be?

The next phase of your New Kid group bonding should be a brain**storming** session. At this stage it's necessary to decide:

- Who is going to be leader? (Just because you're New Kid, and it's your initiative, it doesn't follow that it has to be you.)
- What powers should they have?

- How will the group resolve conflict if more than one person is an equally strong candidate for leader?
- Should dissent be encouraged or discouraged?
- How will group differences be resolved—compromise, formal voting?
- How are strong feelings going to be dealt with?

Other less contentious issues will also need to be addressed at this stage. For example:
- What are the formal rules?
- What unspoken rules are there—no interruptions, "Chatham House Rule" (a rule to protect speakers' confidentiality and encourage free discussion), etc.?
- Are minutes to be taken?
- How far can individuals follow their own interests without diluting the strength of the group?

As you can see, there's plenty for any keen New Kid communication ace to get to grips with here.

The operational stage of the group communication process is called **performing**. To be effective, focus on the specific objectives:
- How is the group going to set about achieving them?
- What responsibilities does each member have?
- Do they understand them clearly?
- How can the group make the time spent together more
- enjoyable?
- Are there plans to socialize?
- How can each member best show support for others and commitment to the group as a whole?

If the group is meeting for a finite purpose—for example, to organize a fundraising event—it's important to celebrate at the end of the process, once the goal has been achieved. As the New Kid, if you're still trying to focus attention on your own achievements, you could arrange a de-briefing session and some form of publicity, internal or external. Recognition of achievement is essential for the whole group if the process is to be considered a success. As for you, your reputation as an effective New Kid communicator will be assured.

(There's more on "Forming/Storming/Performing" in the next chapter.)

INSTIGATOR OR LEADER?

Successful group communication is dependent on having an effective leader. New Kids can make good leaders provided they make sure that everyone who needs to express an opinion has the opportunity to do so. New Kids could be at a bit of a disadvantage here, because they may not know which members of the group are worth listening to, which need to be kept from dominating the proceedings, and which are so reticent that they need to be encouraged to contribute.

As New Kid group leader you should see to it that all subjects are fully explored and that the actions required are clear to everyone. Appoint someone to be accountable for each action point discussed. If obstacles need to be overcome, the group should be encouraged by you as leader to make sure they are surmountable. If solutions are not immediate, the New Kid leader should push for further exploration of the problems. Where choices have to be made, you should present this as an opportunity, not as a difficulty.

Any New Kid who has the ability to be a skilled group communicator will be able to build effective relationships with every member of the group. This is perfect for your strategy to become noticed by the hierarchy in the most positive way. Show that you're willing to accept criticism when it's justified. No one likes "little people" who can't cope with things not going their way. Allow outsiders to join the group to assist in problem solving if appropriate. Open up areas of impasse by canvassing members to offer their perspective on the issue.

THE POWER OF THE PEN

Written communication is more difficult than face-to-face communication. This is particularly so for New Kids. Why do you think this is? It's essentially because you have no control over the reader's reaction.

As a New Kid you may not know, or even have met, the recipient of the communication. What sort of person they are, whether they like reading letters, emails, reports, faxes, is sheer guesswork. If your aim is to grab and keep your reader's attention, as New Kid you have no physical signs (being able to see their facial expressions) or information (knowing something about them) to guide you. Be careful.

Clarity is where it starts and ends in written communication. It will earn you respect as a New Kid, and is a powerful method of persuasion. By writing exactly what you want succinctly and precisely, and expressing it in an interesting and pleasant manner, you'll certainly achieve your objective, which is to be noticed in a positive way.

What else do you want to achieve from your written communication, in addition to getting the reader's attention? A response, of course! You don't want the recipient merely to read it, note it, and file it. If they respond, that's a positive result. Being new in your job, you'll probably be extremely busy. The busier you are, the more attention you should pay to your written communications.

> The first rule of communication is to have something to say. New Kids should know the reason for the communication, and be able to express it clearly.

Give some thought to your readers too:
- Are they young/old, formal/informal, educated/uneducated?
- What structure will you need to use in order to get your message across?
- Would it help to illustrate your message with a "case study"?

Pay attention to the length of the communication. It's far easier to write a long letter than a short one. One page of A4 is the ideal length for most communications. Additional information can always be included as an appendix.

If it's a complex subject and you as New Kid are unsure of how to make an impact, try summarizing. This can be included at the beginning in the form of a bullet-point synopsis and introduction. Or it can come at the end as an overview, recapping points made in the body of the text.

You may take the view (as many journalists do) that the reader will scan only the first and last paragraphs of an article. If this is so, then it's worth investing some time in getting the synopsis right. New Kid communicators should make the end summary all-encompassing. You can then safely assume that even if your reader only has time to get through the last paragraph, they'll understand enough of the subject to know what's going on.

COMMUNICATING AND TECHNOLOGY

The purpose of written communication (of whatever form) is to convey facts. This is important. Distinguish between facts and assumptions. Support factual material with figures, examples, and other material (preferably in the form of appendices). New Kids could be at a disadvantage here, because they may not know where to source the additional information.

If the communication involves numerical information, one way of making this clearer is to include comparisons. ("This year's profits are £5 million, a considerable increase on last year's £1.5 million.") Graphics are now highly sophisticated and are the norm in most company's reports. Pictures, charts, or diagrams often speak louder than words and are powerful communication tools.

Whatever form of communication you're using, make sure that what you write is appropriate to it. For example, the more formal the letter, the less colloquial the language should be. With emails, it's possible to take a more relaxed approach to language. But rules of the workplace should be noted and followed. It's all too easy for the eager New Kid to rush into print and live to regret it. Most companies have a house style that is adhered to not only in their publicity material and website but also in communication.

BLOGGING

Web logging, or "blogging," is the new kid on the media block, and has its own language. There has been a rise in the popularity of business blogs recently. For those who are not regular users, the term "blog" means a Web log—a journal that is available on the Web. It's a community-oriented website that invites participation and collaboration between authors of the site and its readers.

"Bloggers" are those who indulge in the activity of "blogging." A blog is a series of updated posts on a Web page in the form of a calendar or journal, almost always in chronological order. Blogs are now part of mainstream business communications, and some organizations use them to develop relationships with customers and outsmart their competitors.

Because blogs are opinion-based, they reflect the writer's personality, interests, and style. They're written in the first person, informal, and unedited. They do not suit conservative organizations, but are widely used by companies who value freedom of thought and informal communication of ideas. "Phlogging" (posting of photos) and "vlogging" (posting of videos) are variations on the same theme.

> **Beware of disclosing confidential information about your employer, and of criticizing colleagues or the organization (either internally or externally), even if it's unintentional.**

New Kid employees should remember that employers don't like this at all, and that there have been a number of recent reports of people being fired for blogging. New Kid would-be bloggers should check company policy before starting. Most companies will have an established code as to what is acceptable, what topics are off limits, and what the consequences are if these rules are breached. Don't blog in company time if this is not allowed: you would simply be inviting a reprimand, or running the risk of the termination of your employment.

If you're invited to contribute—as New Kid blogging expert—to the feedback of a conference or seminar, be upfront and ask your boss if they agree to your taking part. Blogging is an Internet extension of your own voice, so you shouldn't write anything you wouldn't be prepared to say in public. In the context of your business environment, restraint and discretion are paramount. It's sometimes difficult to play safe and still have something interesting to say, but to be controversial without being offensive should be the aim.

A final word on written communications for all New Kids: be sure to make recommendations or draw a conclusion. Whether this is a call to action or a clarification of what happens next, don't infuriate your readers by forcing them to guess. Making recommendations or drawing conclusions brings the communication to an effective close. Whether or not everyone will agree with them is not the point. If the communication is not pulled together in this way, it fails to make an impact. Recommendations and conclusions don't have to be 100 percent right: they just need to be there.

I KNOW YOU HEARD WHAT I SAID, BUT DID YOU UNDERSTAND WHAT I MEANT?

Communicating clearly is our aim. But what about "other people"? Should you as New Kid bother about understanding them? Emphatically—yes! Knowing how to relate to others is an essential aspect of being a successful New Kid in the workplace. It is vital to build relationships with others if you're going to communicate effectively. At work you are probably involved with a wide range of people whose ages, abilities, and cultures vary hugely. So, how do you start understanding them better in order to be able to communicate effectively?

The secret is simply this: make the other person feel important and respected. One of the strongest human urges is the desire to be seen as important. How do you feel when you are complimented and appreciated? Doesn't a warm glow spread through you? Don't you feel as if you were basking in a ray of sunshine?

If you can make other people feel that way, you'll have learned the most important lesson in the art of communication. The desire of our fellow human beings to be appreciated can be likened to an ongoing hunger, a craving that demands perpetual satisfaction. If you can learn to satisfy this craving, you'll have the art of effective communication in the bag. New Kid, your success is also in the bag!

The ability to arouse enthusiasm in people is a great asset, and the way to get the best out of people is by appreciating and encouraging them. It gives them the incentive to succeed. One of the best ways to do this is to avoid criticizing people.

As a New Kid, you are currently sensitive to criticism yourself and want to create the best possible impression. It follows that you should at all costs avoid belittling other people and their efforts. At a stroke, it kills ambition, destroys motivation, and tests loyalty. It will also undermine confidence, and work may suffer as a consequence. Most people, whether junior or senior, will make a greater effort and do better work in an atmosphere of approval.

An important aspect of communication that is often overlooked is kindness. This is just as relevant in the workplace as it is in our personal and social lives. It inspires loyalty, it motivates, and it encourages. It costs very little to deal with people in a courteous, polite, and compassionate manner.

As a New Kid tactic, it's a sure-fire winner. It earns you respect from all sides, as well as up and down the company hierarchy. Good communication means not taking people for granted. There is nothing worse for any company, or any manager of staff, than having an unmotivated and disgruntled workforce.

Consideration of the other party is paramount when it comes to successful communication. Without appreciation, our self-esteem is denied the nourishment it needs. We're not talking about flattery here—that is quite a different thing. Flattery can be insincere whereas appreciation is sincere.

It's also important for New Kids to remember how easy it is for colleagues and staff to see when you're being insincere. If you can avoid thinking about your own perspective and look for good in others, you'll be able to give honest and sincere appreciation. Praise works wonders, and if you can praise someone's efforts or achievements in public, so much the better.

At work as well as out of the office, people are primarily interested in what they want. One successful way of communicating with colleagues and staff is to find out what they want and help them to get it.

> **Effective communicators are also persuaders. In dealing with staff relationships, the first thing New Kids should do is to arouse in the other person a desire to do something.**

Ask yourself, how can I, as a new member of staff, make this person want to do something? The secret of successful persuasion is the ability to see things from the other person's point of view as well as from your own. This is not manipulation, but a desire to get a win-win situation from every act of communication.

So, don't criticize, give sincere appreciation, and be genuinely interested in the other person's point of view. If you have no interest in the other person and can't—or won't—try to put yourself in their shoes, you will, as a New Kid, have great difficulty in communicating effectively.

Another good idea when communicating with people in the early days of your new position is to start with a smile. This is of course most easily done when dealing with someone face to face, but even in written communications it's possible (with care) to introduce a humorous tone. Charm and good humor will make people like you.

If you're able to do this, people will react favorably toward you and more readily accept the message you are trying to convey. Where possible, make it personal. Remembering people's names is an essential skill, particularly for New Kids. This impresses everyone and will most likely get you a positive response.

What we're talking about here is more than just communication skills: it's good manners. Being polite to colleagues will get you further and faster in your new job than anything else.

> **!** Always listen. Listening skills are essential for all New Kids. It's far better to be a good listener than a good talker.

❝ No man ever listened himself out of a job. **❞**

Calvin Coolidge

Step 06

Do You Wanna Be In My Gang? Being Part Of The Team

> **"** Coming together is a beginning; keeping together is progress; working together is success. **"**
>
> *Henry Ford*

You're the New Kid on the Block, the newest member of the team or department, and an unknown quantity. How scary is that? What you probably want to do most at this moment is win the hearts and minds of the people you work with. This is not just for survival— although it would make life a lot easier—but because you are keen to succeed and get one of the steepest parts of the learning curve over and done with.

Observations of an oldish New Kid on the Block, Angela, who re-entered the workplace at the age of 50 (after a gap of almost 30 years in which she raised her family) as a case officer for the Social Services:

"The important thing to remember when joining a team is to study the dynamics. Don't immediately put forward what seems to you a common-sense way of doing things, especially when dealing with outside agencies. Three weeks in the job will reveal why such a process may or may not be followed. You can then display your brilliance.

> "Refrain from 'in my last position'-type remarks. Every time you use the words, 'This is the way we did it at my last place of work,' it could be construed as criticism. However well-intentioned, it will seem like a put-down to new colleagues. They may have taken you on because you did so well in your last job, and your experience may be second to none, but all they will hear is New Kid saying, 'We did it better there than you are doing it here.'
>
> "Always ask, if you don't know or are in doubt. Colleagues are glad to help—though not when they're in the middle of a crisis.
>
> "If you have the misfortune to join a team in the middle of a rift (and they do occur from time to time, even in the best-run organizations), don't say, 'It seems to me...,' but rather, 'Oh dear!' It's a very useful, defusing phrase and invariably raises a smile."

Becoming a recognized team player is something you should and must do—without delay. You won't achieve this by being aloof. If you want to move with the crowd, the best you can do is:
- Show leadership qualities
- Get involved
- Be willing to get your hands dirty (regularly)
- Know what's going on so that you are able to do all this

People support those who seem to understand their situation. (We're back to communication skills here—see Step 5.) If, as a New Kid, you can show that you have experience of being a team player, most people will readily accept you. It's then up to you to make sure you can genuinely play your part and become a willing and active participant.

One way of quickly winning hearts and minds as the New Kid is to help out when a crisis strikes. People will like it if you pitch in when there's an emergency. In an "all hands to the pumps" situation, don't hang back. Get stuck in and don't pick the easiest (i.e. the cleanest) task. There's nothing more helpful toward gaining respect from other team members than willingly taking a turn at making the tea, or refueling the photocopier.

> **Aim to become part of the team sooner rather than later.**

There was recently a panic-station call at an office I work in. The papers for the annual general meeting had to go out. It was late afternoon and the post was about to be collected. The whole department got together and stuffed close to 1,000 envelopes in about an hour. It was a team effort and the job got done in the shortest time ever. "What fantastic stuffers you all are," said the Director General, as he came back to the

> office with a huge bag of doughnuts. It was great for group morale. He was the New Kid in this illustration, having been in post for only a couple of months. But recognizing the value of the team effort, he'd gone down to the bakery and bought us our reward.

MEETING THE TEAM

You may, as part of the interview process for your new job, have been asked to meet the team you'll be working with. If you haven't been in this situation before, how should you handle it?

One way is simply to treat it like another interview. Be as professional as you can and ask questions. The team will be glad to tell you what you need to know.

Meeting the team isn't just a matter of quickly sizing people up—it can actually be very useful. The key to it is to be relaxed. Most of the team will be your future peers, and they'll be checking you out just as much as you'll be scrutinizing them. The team could ask you all sorts of questions—be sure to make the most of the opportunity to be equally inquisitive and observant.

If you ask team members about their work, you'll see how they interact with each other. If you can figure out how the hierarchy operates, it will be a help. For instance, is everyone equal? Or is there someone who is very much the "Top Dog"?

If you're joining a big team, they'll be thinking about how your skills can bring an overall improvement to the set-up. People look at New Kids to see how their presence can help them. Some team members may have different expectations or needs.

This meeting is a two-way process. You want to make a strong impression, but trying too hard and not being yourself is not a good idea. Adapt your behavior, by all means. After all, this process is about matching.

If after the initial meeting you have a few worries, ask your boss how you're likely to fit in with the team. If they've had any feedback from team members, they should use this opportunity to share it with you.

WORKING TOGETHER

As New Kid, you may be new to the experience of working as part of a team, in which case it will help if you make this clear early on. If the rest of the team are aware of it, they'll give you some help and support. Becoming part of a team, as the New Kid, means becoming involved with everyone in a positive way. Interacting with the rest of the team and being a "player" ensures that together you all succeed.

> Ray works for a global construction company and looks after multi-million-dollar development projects. His advice for New Kids everywhere:
>
> "The most important things to identify when you're a New Kid on the Block are the office politics and the personalities of your new colleagues. Remember that everyone has an agenda. It may be geared to their beliefs, childhood experiences, home life, early days at school, or working environment.

"People often try to influence your decisions while you're a New Kid, to suit their own ego. The key is to identify all the issues— quickly—remain neutral, and sidestep the arrows.

"First of all, New Kids need to identify what's required of them by their immediate boss, by their boss's boss, and by the company as a whole. They must then work single-mindedly to achieve their goals. This is sometimes at the expense of the mounds of reports, paperwork, and nowadays emails that seem to sap the very life-blood of an organization.

"If you can set out your stall and ensure that you have the ability to deliver what you say you'll deliver, you'll succeed. Of paramount importance is that you have the respect and support of your boss.

"Much depends on your age, as New Kid. The older you are, hopefully the wiser you've become and the more credibility you'll have.

"Finally, think about your skills levels. If there are things you love and things you hate with a passion, try to address those that repel. Otherwise, get someone better suited to them than you to take them on. In a professional organization, not being brilliant at everything is not regarded as a crime. Not being honest and then failing in your task is."

> The most important thing in life is to be honest with yourself and with others.

The organizational structure of a team is important. Who does what, how one job relates to another, the lines of reporting and communication—all affect effectiveness. This is something to assess early on and monitor on a regular basis.

Whether you're a team player or a team leader, here are a few points about how teams should work:

- The team structure should fit the tasks to be done
- Any changes should be made on the basis of careful consideration
- Those responsible for the changes should express them in a positive way, otherwise the changes may be viewed with suspicion
- The team leader should keep things under review to ensure that there continues to be a good "fit" between the team and its task (external as well as internal changes or pressures can affect this)
- Teams sometimes need a bit of fine-tuning—keep an eye on tasks, individuals, and the team as a whole

Any anomalies in the way people are organized, no matter how slight, can easily dilute overall effectiveness. New Kid team leaders should not introduce change for its own sake, but neither should they expect things to remain unchanged forever.

GROUP DYNAMICS

A quick and simple way for New Kids involved in team work for the first time to remember the dynamic process of working on a project with a group is to think of the following five words: forming, norming, storming, performing, mourning.

- **Forming:** The group has to get together and agree the way forward. Often there's a common cause or goal that starts the process of cohesion
- **Norming:** When the group has agreed the way forward and resolved the structure of working together, a working relationship is established
- **Storming:** As the group settles down to its task, differing opinions, styles, and ways of working become apparent and friction appears. This needs to be addressed
- **Performing:** As the working relationship matures, and everyone in the team comes to have trust and faith in each other and in the team as a whole, they perform at their best
- **Mourning:** This fifth step is often overlooked, but when a process of change comes to an end there may be a sense of anti-climax and loss, rather than celebration of a job well done. This could be the case, for example, if the change has meant redundancies or relocation

If you've become part of a team in your new job, where are you in the various stages of team development? Keep this exercise in mind and review your progress from time to time. If a new person enters the team, or other factors relating to the project suddenly appear, you may find that the group has to re-form, norm, and storm all over again to get the performing to its best level.

SELF-SUFFICIENCY AND GROUP DYNAMICS

If you organize things so that people are suitably self-sufficient it saves time and promotes goodwill. Remember that having responsibility is motivational—people tend to do best those things for which they see themselves as having personal responsibility.

This means thinking in terms of two distinct levels of self-sufficiency in the way people work:

- **Involvement**
  First, it's necessary to create involvement through, for example, consultation, giving good information, making it clear that suggestions are welcome and that experiment and change are seen as a good thing. This provides an opportunity to contribute beyond the base job

- **Empowerment**
  This goes beyond simple involvement. Empowerment gives people the authority to be self-sufficient (making your own decisions) on an ongoing basis. In a sense, empowerment creates a culture of involvement and gives it momentum

THE POWER OF RESPONSIBILITY

Together involvement and empowerment create an environment in which people can take responsibility for their own actions.

> **!** Responsibility can't be given—it can only be taken. It is thus only the opportunity to take it that can be given.

Creating a situation in which people take responsibility for their work demands:
- Clear objectives (people should know exactly what they have to do and why)
- Good communication
- Motivation (to show the desirability of taking responsibility for the individual as well as the organization)
- Trust (having created such a situation, you, as New Kid team leader, have to let people get on with things)

A team of people enjoying involvement in what they do, and having the authority to make decisions and get the job done, is the best recipe for successful management and a healthy and contented workforce.

STRENGTHENING THE TEAM
To recap for a moment, for New Kids everywhere, a successful team is one that:
- Is set up right
- Responds to the responsibility it has for the task
- Seeks for constant improvement (and never gets stuck "on the tramlines")
- Sees its manager as a fundamental element in its success

A real team will do better, and is more likely to go on doing better, than a group of co-workers who have merely been "told what to do." You, New Kid team leader, have a role as catalyst—constantly helping the team to keep up with events, to change in light of those events, and to succeed because it's always configured for success.

MOTIVATION—A BRIEF OVERVIEW

New Kid managers should know something about the way motivation works. The key is affecting the "motivational climate" by taking action to:

- **Reduce negative influences**

  Many things can have an adverse effect on the way people feel about their jobs. These include company policy and administrative processes, supervision (that's you, unless you're careful!), working conditions, salary, relationships with peers (and others), the impact of work on personal life, and status. Action is necessary in all these areas to reduce the potential for negative feelings

- **Increase** positive influences

  Here specific inputs can strengthen positive feelings. These can be categorized under the following headings: achievement, recognition, the work itself, responsibility, advancement, and growth

There are many ways of contributing to good motivation—from ensuring that a system is as convenient to people as possible to just saying, "Well done" sufficiently often.

The state of motivation of a group or individual can be likened to a balance. There are pluses on one side and minuses on the other. All vary in size. The net effect of all the influences at a particular time determines the state of the balance and whether things are seen as positive or negative overall.

Changing the balance is thus a matter of detail, where, for example, several small positive factors might outweigh what is seen as a major source of dissatisfaction.

MOTIVATING THE TEAM

"United we stand, divided we fall" is an expression that comes to mind when considering the structure of teams. If, as a New Kid team manager, you can involve people on broad issues, you'll find this is motivational for all concerned.

> Don't underestimate your staff. Their views can enhance everything—
> methods, standards, processes, and overall effectiveness.

Resolve now that you'll make motivation a priority. Motivation makes a difference—a big difference. People perform better when they feel positive about their job. You are the New Kid motivator, so you must:
- Recognize that active motivation is necessary
- Resolve to spend regular time on it

- Not chase after magic formulas that will make it easy (there aren't any)
- Give attention to the detail
- Remember that you succeed by creating an impact that is cumulative in effect and tailored to your team members

Your intention should be to make people feel, both individually and as a group, that they're special. This is the first step to making sure that what they do is special.

As team leader, or manager, you're not paid to have all the ideas. You are paid, however, to make sure that there are enough ideas to make things work and continue working. New Kid managers should make use of their teams or sections and make it clear to them that they want and value their contributions.

OBTAINING SIGNIFICANT MOTIVATIONAL RESULTS

New Kid team leaders need to make it clear from the outset that the way group members feel about their work is important to them:

- **Take the motivational temperature.** Find out how people feel now—this is what you have to work on
- **Consider the motivational implications of everything you do.** Whenever you put a new system in place, make a change, or set up a new regular meeting, ask yourself: What will people think about it? Will they see it as positive?

- **Never be censorious.** Don't judge other people's motivation by your own feelings. Maybe they worry about things that strike you as silly or unnecessary—so be it. The job is to deal with it, not to rule it out as insignificant

> Making motivation a key part of your management style will stand you in good stead. If you care about people, it will show.

GETTING THE BEST FROM THE TEAM

Be aware that your effectiveness as New Kid depends on your team and on the interaction of three separate factors. If you're a New Kid team leader, you must:

- Ensure continual task achievement
- Meet the needs of the group
- Meet the needs of individual group members

This balance must always be kept in mind (though some compromise may be necessary). As New Kid, your own contribution to getting things done is ideally approached systematically:

- Make sure you know exactly what the tasks are
- Understand how they relate to the objectives of the organization (short- and long-term)
- Plan how they can be achieved
- Identify and provide the resources needed

- Create a team structure and organization that facilitates effective action
- Monitor progress as necessary during task completion
- Evaluate results, compare with objectives, and fine-tune action and method for the future

The following three checklists can be used in conjunction with what has been set out above. These will not only be of use to team leaders, but should also help New Kids to integrate into the group.

Checklist 1: Achieving the task
Ask yourself as New Kid:
- Am I clear about my own responsibilities?
- Am I clear about the department's agreed objectives?
- Do I have a plan for achieving these objectives?
- Are jobs best structured to achieve what is required?
- Do we have the necessary working conditions and resources?
- Are others clear about their personal targets?
- Are the group competencies as they should be?
- Are we focused on priorities?
- Is my own contribution well-organized?
- Do I have the information necessary to monitor progress?
- Is management continuity (in my absence) assured?

- Am I looking sufficiently far ahead and seeing the broad picture?
- Do I set a good example?

Checklist 2: Team maintenance

To ensure that the whole team is pulling together toward individual and joint objectives, ask yourself: Do I, as New Kid team leader:

- Set team objectives clearly and make sure that they're understood?
- Ensure that standards (and the consequences of not meeting them) are understood?
- Find opportunities to create team-working?
- Minimize dissatisfactions?
- Seek and welcome new ideas?
- Consult appropriately and sufficiently often?
- Keep people fully informed (about the short and the long term)?
- Reflect the team's views in dealing with senior management?
- Reflect organizational policy in team objectives?

An analytical approach to these areas is fundamental to making the team operation work effectively—and thus to handling tasks effectively.

Checklist 3: Meeting individual needs

Ask yourself if individual members of the team (particularly any New Kid members):

- Derive a sense of personal achievement from what they do and the contribution it makes
- Feel that their jobs are challenging and match their capabilities
- Receive suitable recognition for what they do
- Have control of the areas of work for which they are accountable
- Feel that they're advancing in terms of experience and ability

It's worth thinking through what you need to ask in terms of your own particular team and any new players that may recently have joined.

THE POWER OF CONSISTENCY

> People manage to work successfully with all kinds of colleagues—the tough and the tender. Nothing throws them more, however, than a New Kid team member who runs hot and cold.

This problem is at its worst when it's the team leader who acts inconsistently. A leader who is sweetness and light one minute (ready to listen and consult) and doom and gloom the next (demanding that people "do as I say") is extremely difficult to work with.

At first you may need to experiment a little with different approaches. Thereafter, you should try to adopt a consistent style in dealing with your team:

- Let people know that you'll always make time for them (soon, at an agreed time, if not instantly)
- Make it clear that you never prevaricate. Decisions may not be made instantly if they need thought or consultation, but neither will they be endlessly avoided. If there must be some delay, tell people why and when things will be settled—and deliver on your promises
- Make sure people understand how you approach things and what your attitude is to problems, opportunities, and so on. While individual solutions may—doubtless should—be different, your method and style of going about things should be largely a known quantity

People like to know where they are, and work better when they do.

Step 07

New Kids Need Friends: How To Win Friends And Influence People

> **❝** Be nice to people on your way up because you'll meet 'em on your way down. **❞**
>
> *Wilson Mizner*

If you haven't read the famous book *How To Win Friends and Influence People* written by Dale Carnegie in the early part of the last century, it's still available and well worth browsing through. I have often thought that a book entitled "How not to irritate people" would be quite useful, and maybe one day I'll write it.

Certainly for New Kids there is nothing more important than being able to make friends in the first few days of your new job. A friendly wave or smile as you enter your place of work in the morning can transform it for you in an instant.

Let's begin by considering some of the types of people you could be dealing with. Who have you met so far in the company? Where do they fit in the office hierarchy? If you can already identify them and have an idea of their job titles and what they do, you won't waste valuable time and resources dealing with them in the wrong way.

Every New Kid should understand the importance of human behavior.

> **"Study human behavior. Every business solution comes down to influencing people."**
>
> *Sir John Collins, Chairman of Dixons Group, Ex-Chairman of National Power*

When you arrived at your new job, you were probably introduced to a lot of people in a short space of time. If you were able to think coherently (and were not panicking too much about the impression you were creating), hopefully you made some mental notes.

For instance, did you note which of your immediate colleagues seemed genuinely pleased to meet you when you were introduced? While you're still feeling a bit apprehensive about engaging colleagues in conversation or asking them if you might join them for lunch, it would make sense to begin with these.

LOOK AROUND YOU FIRST

Who are the real decision makers in the company (not those on the organizational chart but those that wield major influence in the boardroom)?

What is the basis of their power? Is it time spent in the company, or previous relationships with one or more members of the board, or something else?

Remember, everyone in the company is important. Don't underestimate someone just because they are junior, as their power base may be much greater than you think.

> In his new position as Finance Director, Leslie found that a certain lady had a direct route to the board and always knew what was going on well in advance of her more senior colleagues. How? She had worked for the company for many years and had been of great assistance to the CEO (through being a listening ear) when his wife had died several years previously. He subsequently made sure she was protected—and in the know! Leslie says it took him some time to find this out and he nearly made some costly mistakes in the meantime.

No doubt you will, as an excellent New Kid, begin a contacts database, which will include your colleagues, staff, team members, and superiors. You could usefully spend a bit of time figuring out what makes them "tick." If you can develop the habit of doing this when you meet people, you'll be amazed how easily and successfully you can "connect."

Once you've identified a particular type, you'll find that you meet other people who remind you of them. Whether the likeness is physical or a matter of personality, you'll probably know instinctively how they'll react when you speak to them, and how to "get on their wavelength."

> **!** Companies prosper when staff are genuinely interested in their colleagues.

When trying to build relationships with people, it's important to remember that the process requires confidence. Some people are naturally reticent while others are born extroverts. People who are skilled at this show certain traits:

- They treat everyone as if they were interesting, special, and likable
- They use good eye contact and positive body language
- They introduce people to each other effortlessly, remembering names and personal details

In other words, they have charm.

GO ON A CHARM OFFENSIVE

> **!** Charm is contagious—you come across as being generous and will be able to build self-esteem in others.

Be a charmer! This is excellent advice for all New Kids. You probably recall having met someone like this already in your career. When you were introduced, they smiled, entered into conversation easily, and drew you out. They probably asked you questions about yourself, and listened to what you said. In essence, they made you feel important. When you parted, you probably thought to yourself, What a great person!

Not only is it easy to be in their company, but such people are at ease with themselves. Am I describing someone you know, or the person you'd like to be?

New Kids, remember that if you're a bit nervous in your first few days, you may not be coming across as well as you should. To be a charmer, you should be confident and assertive, but not arrogant, vain, or conceited.

Charmers are enthusiastic and have broad horizons. Above all, they're curious, and that is something New Kids can certainly identify with. Charmers:

- Ask a lot of questions
- Empathize
- Are responsive to situations and circumstances
- Have a good sense of humor
- Are a bit self-deprecating, if appropriate
- Have the ability to "mirror" people
- Are good listeners

MASTERING THE ART OF GOOD QUESTIONING

This is perhaps the single most powerful tool in the art of making friends (particularly in the workplace) and is extremely important for New Kids everywhere.

Asking good questions shows that you're interested in the other person. It's best to ask open questions, ones that don't require the answer yes or no.

> **!** Good questions build good relationships. They indicate that you care about the other person and their situation. The more questions you ask, the more you are encouraging the other person to trust you.

Good questions convey competence, sincerity, and sympathy. You need to practice the art of listening too. New Kids should pay attention to what colleagues say and note this information for future use.

If someone tells you they're looking forward to going to a particular play at the weekend and the next time you meet them you ask if they enjoyed it (bonus points awarded if you remember the name of the play!), they'll be impressed and you'll rise high in their estimation.

INTERACTION

New Kids should try to observe the workplace atmosphere:
- How do staff members behave toward one another?
- Do colleagues interact easily and with openness?

Remember, anxieties and insecurities will hinder good communication. If as a New Kid you feel inadequate and of little value, you'll have difficulty in approaching people. This should pass after a few days. The best advice is to take it slowly and hold back until you feel confident to make a start.

> **People tend to be one of two types—extrovert or introvert, those who are people-oriented or those who are highly task-aware.**

In your new job you'll note that the latter type often find it difficult to appreciate the value of personal relationships. Have you identified anyone like this yet? They would rather sit at their desk, staring at the computer screen all day than get up and interact. This doesn't mean that they're workaholics—probably just that they're shy and that their social skills are weak.

As a New Kid you are much more likely to receive an email request from such people than a personal approach, even if they're sitting at the next desk. They are the ones who avoid getting coffee from the machine. They might even have their own flask with them. They'll do anything to avoid having to strike up a conversation with a colleague.

People like this do exist. I've worked with some of them and it's staggering what lengths they'll go to, to keep themselves to themselves. Sometimes they try to cover it up by saying they haven't got time to chat and there's too much gossiping anyway.

> **Don't underestimate the importance of a bit of staff bonding. It goes a long way to enhancing goodwill among team members and colleagues.**

Have you found out yet how much staff members in your new office really know about each other? Have you identified the key people to network with in your organization?

It will probably take a bit of time to figure out which ones are the decision makers, the movers and shakers, the influential persuaders. But it's also important to understand how all the others fit into the food chain.

You may not have much time to think about this at the moment, but remember that your colleagues and your boss are only human beings. They have hopes, fears, and insecurities, like you. Sometimes they need nurturing too.

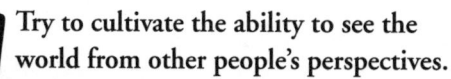

! Try to cultivate the ability to see the world from other people's perspectives.
● Find out how your new boss and colleagues prefer to work.

IDENTIFYING KEY PLAYERS

It's a common assumption (you'd be surprised just how common) that influential people are those who hold high office. It isn't necessarily so. If you have a wide range of contacts, some of whom go back a number of years, you'll find that a number of them are not in elevated positions and yet wield considerable power.

For New Kids, here are two examples:

This is taken from Making Management Simple (How To Books, 2005). Thanks to Nicola Stevens.

The board of a company decided that, as part of their modernization program, they needed to link two buildings that were separated by a busy road. They commissioned architects and consultants to apply to the local planning department to build a bridge between the two factories. The application was refused. They spent many hours and a great deal of money researching other solutions but came up with none. The board and the consultants were stuck.

One morning the chairman of the board was driving to work, and some way ahead of him saw the caretaker on the other side of the road. The man disappeared into the building, but by the time the chairman passed the spot he saw to his amazement that the caretaker was now standing on his side of the road. He stopped his car and shouted to the caretaker, "How did you do that—get from one side of the road to the other without walking across?" Answer? There was an underground maintenance passage. For some reason it was not on the site plans, but it was in daily use by a small section of the workforce.

Moral: Never be too proud to ask or underestimate the knowledge and experience of every single person you work with.

> Andrew used to work for a global company that was hierarchical in its approach. One day he needed the advice of the chairman on a particular matter. He went through the usual channels and asked the chairman's PA if he could possibly see him for ten minutes. She replied that he would not be available for two weeks.
>
> Andrew knew the decision could not wait, so he went to find the chairman's chauffeur, Charles. He found him in the company canteen and bought him a cup of coffee. In the course of the ensuing conversation he asked Charles where the chairman was. Charles told Andrew he was driving the chairman to the airport that afternoon at 3.00 p.m., and that if Andrew wanted to see him he should wait by the main entrance. Andrew was at the door at the appointed time. He spoke to the chairman, who invited him to ride with him to the airport so that he could give the matter some consideration. The advice was given and the problem solved.

! Small talk can make a big difference!

- Be prepared to think laterally in order to solve problems
- Remember that a small piece of information can make a big difference

- Forging powerful connections doesn't just mean getting to know "the great and the good"
- Pay attention to everyone—and discover their individual strengths
- Sometimes a valuable piece of information can come from the most unlikely source

You'll soon recognize the following types:

MOVERS AND SHAKERS

These usually far exceed the boundaries of their office positions. For New Kids, it's wise to find out who they are as soon as you can. You won't have trouble spotting them because they make it their business to see and be seen. It's important to keep track of Movers and Shakers—you never know where they're going to turn up next.

CORPORATE CITIZENS

These are the hard-working, non-political types, who are great sources of information and advice on almost every aspect of the organization. They've probably been around for quite a while and know the inside and outside of the company, their department, and most of its staff. They probably even know the date of the Chief Executive's wife's birthday. If you as a New Kid nurture them and seek their advice when appropriate, they'll be flattered. Better to ask them than have them say afterward, "If only you'd asked me, I could have told you that . . ."

Keep an eye out for Fire Fighters, Vetoers, and Whiners.

These can be troublesome and difficult to deal with effectively while your learning curve still resembles a sheer rock face.

> **!** If we're here to help others, what are others here for?

Some people you know may be highly task-aware, while others are more people-oriented. You'll build your most valuable connections with people who like dealing with other people. Here are four more types:

ROADRUNNERS

These are usually highly task-aware and will not let anyone, least of all a New Kid, stand in their way of achieving targets. They can be quite dangerous and it's wise to let them pass if you find you're in their way—which you could well be—during your first few weeks in your new job. Watch out, otherwise you could be roughly elbowed aside or, worse still, flattened as they rush past.

RACEHORSES

These people get things done fast but like to ask others to help them. They are perfect to team up with when you're a New Kid because of the accelerated pace at which they work. You'll find yourself flying along—make sure you can keep up. A Racehorse is a valuable asset in any group. They are strong and capable and can achieve great things. But you do need to remain in the saddle— riderless horses can be dangerous! If you're a New Kid team leader, harness them wisely to the right group and you'll have a winning combination.

NEW PUPS

You must know some of these. They are the most people-oriented types and will be extremely eager to please when you're a New Kid. They much prefer to be with others and are no good at working alone. However, they often have fairly low awareness of the importance of getting things done. New Kid managers should watch out—New Pups can spend too much time being helpful and friendly, and are not the best at keeping to deadlines. New Kids, you must watch out, because although charming, friendly, and extremely social, they may hinder your ability to get things done on time.

TOMCATS

These prefer to be left alone to get on with their work. As a New Kid, you'll find them rather difficult to build a rapport with. They're independent, unaware of other people and of the importance of teams. Some of them are eggheads (lonely geniuses) and produce amazing results. They don't mean to be unfriendly—it's just that they're often in a world of their own and happiest in their own company.

PERSUASION TECHNIQUES

Some New Kids may want to use a bit of psychology when dealing with others. There's a theory that people have different energies and are therefore represented by a particular color. Which color are you? And what about your new colleagues? There are four main types:

COOL BLUES

These are usually regarded as the aloof types. They can be cautious, precise, deliberate, and formal. New Kids will find them a bit distant, because they hold off getting close to people (compare Tomcats). If you're trying to work with them, or influence them, you'll need to handle them very carefully.

FIERY REDS

These are pretty much the opposite of the Blues. They're competitive, demanding, determined, and strong-willed. As a New Kid you won't have any trouble spotting them. They'll reach their goals whatever it takes, even if they have to knock you out of the way in order to do so (compare Roadrunners). New Kid Reds might have to tone down their actions if they want to avoid alienating others by rejecting offers of help.

SUNSHINE YELLOWS

These are sociable, dynamic, demonstrative, enthusiastic, and persuasive. If you have Yellows in your group, you'll find they're a great asset. Yellows have natural charisma and are able to shine in any situation. If you're a New Kid Yellow, you'll be at ease in most situations and will find people naturally gravitate toward you. You'll quickly become a valued member of the team, because you'll help keep morale high. No matter how difficult the job is, you try to see things in a positive light.

EARTH GREENS
These are caring, sharing, encouraging, compassionate, and patient individuals. New Kids, you probably know a number of them. You'll find them really kind and helpful—they just can't help it! (Compare New Pups.) If you've got any Greens in your office, they're the ones who will always have the headache tablets, take care of the plants, and remember everyone's birthday.

> ! If you need to get on with people who are not like you, try adopting the chameleon approach—change color to suit the environment you're in.

CAN I BE DIFFERENT?
Is it acceptable to challenge the status quo and offer a new view on the world (part of being the New Kid on the Block)? Or are you expected to listen and learn the value of the existing culture?

What about dress code? Is it formal or informal? Is it the same at internal meetings and meetings with clients?

> Karen works for a media company that has both mainstream and new-wave clients. In the office she knew that the mode was dress-down; for mainstream clients it was business suits (formal) and for the new-wavers it was totally dress-down. As New Kid she found this environment interesting and challenging. She had to try to make sure that meetings with mainstream and newwave clients weren't scheduled on the same day—and it also proved sensible to keep some clothes suitable for each occasion in the office, just in case meetings were fixed at short notice.

WHAT'S YOUR BODY LANGUAGE SAYING?

It's true that we give away a lot about ourselves through our body language, and as a New Kid you'll know that everyone is watching you. If you remember some of the rules, it may help to get you through the first few weeks a bit more easily.

Equally, recognizing and understanding body language is important in business, and paying attention to this may reveal what your colleagues really think about you. Here's a brief summary:

EYES RIGHT

Eye contact is one of the most important aspects of dealing with other people. New Kids, remember when meeting new people that maintaining eye contact shows respect and interest in what they have to say. It's appropriate to keep eye contact for about 60—70 percent of the time here in the West, but of course this differs in other cultures (so pay attention to that). By keeping to the 65 percent ratio you'll be attentive without making others feel self-conscious. If your expression remains riveted to someone's face, they may assume there's something wrong. If you fix your gaze on their lips, it might give the impression that you'd like to kiss them! Maybe New Kids should hold back a bit here.

POSTURING

If you naturally have good posture, New Kid, you'll be giving off the right vibes. Head upright and shoulders erect shows that you're in control, professional, and efficient. Slouching, drooping, shuffling— all of these inhibit breathing and give the impression that you're nervous or uncomfortable.

HEADS UP

The position of your head is a great give-away. When you want to show how confident you are, keep your head level both horizontally and vertically. The straight head position conveys authority and lets people know you want to be taken seriously. When trying to be friendly, or to cultivate people, New Kids should try the tilted head. Just a little to one side or the other, and shift the head at various times during the conversation. This should engage people and show that you're interested in them.

ARMING YOURSELF

Did you realize that arms are a clue as to how open and receptive you are? If your arms are out to the side of the body or behind your back, you'll be showing that you're not scared and can take whatever comes your way. New Kids, if you make big arm movements this will show you are more confident than those who move their arms less. Avoid crossing your arms, as this could be interpreted as showing disapproval or withdrawing from the interchange. You may just be feeling cold, but people may get a different impression.

LEGS

Because they're a long way from the brain, you may have to try harder to control your legs. If you're a nervous New Kid, don't allow your legs to let you down. Keep them as still as possible, particularly on first-impression occasions. When crossing your legs, do you cross ankles or knees, or bring one ankle up to rest on the knee of the other leg? (Ladies, the last is not advisable when wearing a skirt!) Your choice of leg-cross will be determined by comfort and dress; the important thing is that you come across as composed and confident.

HANDS

There are so many gestures—an entire chapter could be devoted to this subject alone. New Kids, just remember that palms up and outward are seen as open and friendly, and palms down as dominant and emphatic, particularly if the arm is held straight with no bending of wrist or forearm. When shaking hands, make the gesture upright and vertical, as this will convey equality.

DISTANCE

This is crucial for New Kids wishing to give off the right signals. Stand too close and you'll be considered pushy and too "in your face." Stand too far away and you'll be judged as aloof or withdrawn. Neither is desirable, so best to watch what others do and see how the group interrelates. If you find that a colleague backs away when you move toward them, this is because they see you as moving into their "comfort zone." New Kids should respect this and back off. You'll soon know when it's appropriate to approach more closely.

EARS

You have two of these; remember to use them. If you keep this in mind, it will help communication with new colleagues.

MOUTH

This is a very expressive part of the body. Lips can be pursed or twisted if you are thinking hard. Mouth clamped shut? Perhaps New Kids wishing to hold back angry comments should do this, even though it may give the impression that you are not pleased. Better that than insulting someone. Smiling is what the mouth is best for, though there are of course different kinds of smile. New Kids wishing to create the feel-good factor should aim for a pleasant friendly smile, as opposed to a crazed manic grin, which could give the wrong impression.

FITTING IN

New Kids who can fit in easily with the pattern at work will find themselves absorbed as a full member of the team quite quickly. Observation is the key here. For example, don't make a lot of noise early in the morning if you see that some of your colleagues prefer to start the day quietly. New Kids whose antennae are properly tuned will be able to pick up on the signals—such as when interruptions are welcome and when not. Make sure you are an office asset and not a distraction.

A "thank you" never comes amiss. If praise is due, then say something—in public, if it can be done appropriately. The results can be dynamic.

While you are trying to build relationships internally, it pays to spend time ascertaining people's likes and dislikes.

Try compiling a "stakeholder map." Make a list of those you need to get to know. Think about the ways in which you could currently make contact with them. Are there other ways of doing so? Have you some idea of how often you should keep in touch with them?

CREATING A VIRTUAL TEAM

! As soon as possible after joining your new company, you should try to identify your own "hot list" of contacts.

Your virtual team consists of your "inner circle" of colleagues who can help you and influence others at times when support is needed. This is not a quick fix, and cannot necessarily be done in the first 100 days of your new position but it's so important to your survival in your job, that you should start work on it as soon as you can.

To begin with, you may well be relying on "old connections" from your previous workplace, education establishment, family, friends, etc.

My inner circle consists of perhaps ten people. They are people I know extremely well and for whom I have a huge amount of respect. Sometimes I get stuck on a particular problem or issue. By calling one or two of them and asking, "What would you do in this situation?" or "Have you ever come up against this?" or "Who would you talk to?" I get a quick injection of common sense, or a radical solution to what I had thought was an insuperable problem.

You'll find there are probably no more than six to ten people who can be included in this close circle of allies. This "virtual team" is an essential aid for New Kids, and it's a "two-way street." This means that, as a New Kid, you need to identify the areas in which you can be supportive and useful to them, and how in turn they can "look out" for you.

When creating your virtual team, you'll need to find people you're actually interested in. It also helps if you understand the work they do and how it impacts on your own job. You will in time get to know their likes and dislikes and be genuinely interested in their success and happiness. If there's a distance issue—that is, if they actually move away from the office you perhaps once shared—you can send regular informative emails, or keep in touch by phone, or arrange to meet up for a coffee and chat when they're visiting.

Members of your virtual team should not only be called on to help with your problems. Wise New Kids, if you want to keep your visibility high, keep them informed about what you're doing, and ask about any new developments in their career as well.

The unique thing about your virtual team is that you'd stick up for them, write a glowing recommendation, support them, listen sympathetically to their concerns, spring into action for them— whatever it takes. In essence, you trust them—because they'd do the same for you.

Step 08

It's Not What You Do, It's The Way That You Do It: Developing Successful Working Relationships

> **“** A wise man will make more opportunities than he finds. **”**
>
> *Francis Bacon*

THE VALUE OF GOSSIP

In some places, where the Protestant version of the work ethic still prevails, the belief is that to chatter is idle. "Shooting the breeze" doesn't get the job done. When you're the New Kid, you should be careful that you aren't seen to be spending most of your time talking to colleagues. However, when your "need to know" is all-important, there's nothing like gossip to help fill the gaps. After all, until you've heard everything, how can you possibly decide how important the information is and whether you need to know it or not!

We might learn a lesson or two from Continental Europe. The first hour in French, Spanish, and Italian offices is spent kissing. In the second you exchange the latest gossip and in the third you go out for coffee and a croissant. Of course, I exaggerate!

> ! Being gossip-averse can be a mistake. Conversation is the way relationships
> ● are formed.

Perhaps I should define "gossip" as useful chat rather than the spreading of malicious rumors about someone's reputation or latest conquest. New Kids, beware! Keep your opinions to yourself. In this context your communication techniques should be firmly switched from "transmit" to "receive."

Relationships between people are a company's greatest asset. If colleagues can't work together, they won't be able to succeed in their job—neither will they have a very pleasant time doing it. New Kids who integrate well and appropriately, who can hold good-quality conversations with co-workers, are valuable to any organization.

> **!** Conversation should not be confused with communication. Communication is about exchanging information, whereas conversation is a creative process and engages people's minds.

Conversations don't stick to agendas; neither do they incorporate jargon or management theory and hype.

Conversation is about connectivity—enabling staff to keep in touch with one another. It's an antidote to stress and other health problems. New Kids who successfully develop good social relationships at work are far less likely to be anxious, stressed, absent, or seeking to move on.

> **!** It's good to talk! Gossip and
> conversation encourage effective
> ● working. Be brave—don't just have a
> solitary coffee and read your emails. Ask a
> colleague to take a break with you and sit
> and chat together for a few minutes.

USING YOUR INTUITION

> I have two good friends who are totally blind. One has been blind from birth, while the other was blinded in an accident at work in his mid-forties. Both of them have an unerring ability to make accurate judgments, particularly when it comes to people. I've told them that they "see" people better than a sighted person, and they reacted in the same way: "Of course we can—we use our third eye."

There's bound to be someone in your new job (or perhaps more than one person) who you'll have some difficulty connecting with as a New Kid. This could prove to be a bit of a stumbling block, particularly if this person is in your direct reporting line. There could be a number of reasons for their reserve, including disappointment at their lack of progress in the office by comparison with yours, or an unhappy home life.

One way of tackling the issue is to pause, to hold back from making any further overtures. If they are continually ignoring or rebuffing your approaches, you have nothing to lose by taking a bit of time over this.

Think about the way this person behaved when you first met them:
- What initial reaction did you get?
- What was their voice like?
- Did they have a firm handshake?
- Did they readily make eye contact with you?

New Kids should pay particular attention to such things. Do you listen to the sound of someone's voice? Do you notice their touch as they shake your hand? Is it strong or weak? Are they tactile or reserved? Do they stand near to you, inappropriately close, or far away?

If you can tune in to people's "vibes" (the "third eye" approach), you'll reduce the likelihood of making incorrect judgments about them. Believe me, this is easy enough to do, particularly when you're a New Kid. Over the years I've made a good few mistakes— some of them rather costly.

> **!** At some time or other in your new job you'll have to deal with difficult people.

One of the best pieces of advice I ever received was from a highly successful finance director. I asked him if there was any particular thing to which he attributed his success. He said he had, early on in his career, developed the combined skills of an acrobat, a diplomat, and a doormat. The key to the issue, he added wryly, was knowing in which order and in what proportion these skills should be used.

If you can work that one out, you're destined to be a high-flier.

ASSERTIVENESS

> When you're new to a job it's particularly difficult if one or two of your colleagues are high-maintenance people (HMPs), or downright bullies. In this situation you should review your assertiveness techniques.

The key to being assertive is managing to leave any difficult situation feeling OK about both yourself and the other person involved.

The aim is a win-win outcome in terms of both self-respect and mutual respect. The bonus is the absence of anxiety afterward. You, New Kid, won't have feelings of guilt, embarrassment, or frustration.

The difference between being aggressive, passive, and assertive is as follows:

- An aggressive response is a put-down. It's a personal attack, tinged with sarcasm and arrogance
- A passive response is your choice not to say or do anything confrontational. But it can leave you feeling frustrated afterward

- An assertive response is a reasonable objection delivered in a polite and positive manner

New Kids are anxious to please. In situations of potential conflict, how do you normally respond? If you're trying to avoid being taken advantage of by the HMPs in your office, you'll need to be able to think on your feet. If you find yourself in a tricky situation, an assertive response is the best one for you, because it's likely to produce a win-win outcome.

Passive behavior gives New Kids no advantage, and you can lose a good deal from behaving aggressively. But what you can gain from being assertive is that you feel good about yourself. You also have the satisfaction of knowing that you've handled a difficult situation correctly. You'll feel no anxiety or guilt. Once you've figured out what the tangible benefits are, it will make you more assertive in future.

Here are some situations and solutions for New Kids to consider:

Situation 1: Your boss asks you to work over the weekend for the second time in a month. You understand the importance of the deadline and, being a New Kid, are anxious to please. But it's your son's fifth birthday and you've promised him you'll be at home to help with his party.

- *Solution A:* You tell your boss you've already done your fair share, having given up your previous weekend. You say it's interfering with your family life and insist that there are other people he should ask

- *Solution B:* You resign yourself to working on your son's birthday. You've now got to go home and explain the situation to your partner and child and then spend the whole of the weekend feeling guilty and resentful
- *Solution C:* You say you have other commitments but offer to come in early on Monday and stay late a couple of evenings if that would help

Situation 2: You've just started working for a company with an established "long-hours culture." This is a new experience for you and it's wearing you out. You decide that if you're going to continue with your job, you need to cut back to a four-day week, and you draw up a proposal to present to your directors. Your proposal is turned down.

- *Solution A:* You plead with them, explaining that the hours you work are making life impossible
- *Solution B:* You threaten to resign if they won't compromise
- *Solution C:* You ask for a detailed explanation as to why your proposal has been rejected. Once you've seen it, you realize that they've had a bad experience in the past with someone who made a similar suggestion. You rework your proposal to counter their objections and reassure them that you won't let them down

Situation 3: In your first departmental meeting, a colleague presents one of your ideas, which you'd discussed with her a couple of days before, as her own.

- *Solution A:* You express disbelief and firmly point out that this was originally your idea. You go on to say that you resent being treated in such an underhand way
- *Solution B:* You say nothing because, as a New Kid, you're worried about causing an argument in front of everyone. But you decide to have a word with her afterward to set the record straight
- *Solution C:* You diplomatically point out that this is something you and she had discussed, because you'd found that this particular idea had worked well in your previous job. You say how pleased you are that she's taken it on board so quickly, and invite her to work with you on the project

Situation 4: In your first week, you have an urgent project to complete. You don't want to let the department down, so you ask your assistant to help you. He says he has an even more important assignment to complete for another partner.

- *Solution A:* You try pulling rank and say there's no way this deadline can be missed. You tell him that he'll have to stay late to do the work and mention that you've never had any difficulty of this sort with staff in previous jobs
- *Solution B:* You try to bribe him to fit your work in—it's something you've done successfully in previous jobs
- *Solution C:* You explain why the work has to be finished today, and offer to speak to someone about the work he'll have to lay aside to help you. You thank him, and tell him you'll repay the favor

OVERCOMING DIFFICULTIES

New kids may well be faced with dilemmas in the first few weeks of taking up their position. This is often exacerbated by their lack of internal knowledge. After all, they've only just begun to understand the complexities of the organization.

> When faced with a difficult situation, it sometimes seems easier to postpone dealing with the issue. Beware: nothing ever gets better by being ignored.

Why is it likely that New Kids will procrastinate when faced with an awkward situation? There are usually three reasons:
- Fear of being ignored
- Fear of being humiliated
- Fear of being rejected

Here are some suggestions New Kids could keep in mind when dealing with situations that require tact and diplomacy:
- **First, acknowledge that there's a problem.** If you check your emotions, body sensations, and thoughts, you'll be in control of yourself. That will help you to take control of the issue
- **Communicate clearly and positively.** If appropriate (and it would be wise, given that you're a New Kid), get support from a colleague or superior

- **Be flexible in your approach and review your goals.** What outcome would be best? What are you realistically likely to achieve?
- **Don't procrastinate.** Act now to confront the challenge. A problem doesn't get any easier to deal with if it's ignored
- **Pay attention when engaging the other party.** Listen—without interrupting. Show that you understand how they feel as well as what they're saying
- **Analyze the problem.** It's crucial to differentiate between facts ("These sales figures are incorrect"), assumptions ("The figures must have been prepared by junior members of staff"), generalities ("You never check your figures"), and emotions ("How can I possibly trust you?")
- **Respond quickly.** If there's any action you can take immediately to make things better, do so. Focus on this rather than on the cause of the problem
- **It's not necessary to take things personally.** Don't give a flat no as an answer and don't apportion blame. It's unwise to make promises you can't keep. If possible, retain a sense of humor— laughter can lower the temperature considerably

> **If you think you're about to lose an argument with a member of your team, do everything in your power to repair the relationship damage before it goes too far. Being able to recover a situation in such a way that no one loses face often leads to stronger and deeper relationships.**

If in the early days of a working relationship you think you may have lost a colleague's trust, lose no time in trying to win back their confidence.

It could be that someone feels slighted because they haven't been consulted about a particular change in working procedures or because their views on how things have been managed in the past haven't been noted.

The lesson for New Kids here is to give advance warning of any changes you wish to make. Ask for team members' views. It's far easier to open up a consultative phase and then, after appropriate consideration, bring about change through reasoned argument than it is to ignore other people's views altogether and insist that they "do as I say." Taking the temperature of the department is a good way to avoid breakdown in communications and relationships. Staff will feel that their fears about change were unwarranted and will be more likely to trust your judgment in future.

> **Never make an enemy when you could create an alliance.**

ANGER MANAGEMENT

Is this going to be a confrontational exchange? I hope not!
- Do you ever get involved in conflict?
- Does your voice sometimes develop a hard edge?
- Have you ever slammed the phone down on someone?
- Do you behave toward others in an adult fashion?
- Does your inner child sometimes escape?

You are bound to encounter someone at work who has a tendency to "throw their rattle out of the pram." New Kids should try to adopt the techniques of a smooth operator. Especially in these first few weeks, you'll need to be able to glide over any rock-strewn path with ease.

Here are some defusing techniques for dealing with angry exchanges:
- **In the first place, stay cool.** You can help or hinder a difficult situation by controlling your voice. It should contain no hint of annoyance, arrogance, or nastiness—only obvious concern for the other party. This will help to transform a battleground into a playground.
- **When someone is angry with you, move toward them verbally.** Your new boss may be incensed about something you've done. Meet them on equal terms. If you're not on the defensive, it will make them less aggressive. If they're raising their voice, lower yours. Use open questions when inquiring about the problem. Suggest some possible solutions. If in difficulty, "suspend reaction." If you don't erupt with

fury, or resort to sarcasm, they can't keep fanning the flames. It's very difficult to keep an argument going single-handedly
- **When it's your turn to respond, stay calm.** One angry person is quite enough. Be sympathetic—show the other person that you understand and are anxious to deal with the problem. Tell them what you're prepared to do about it
- **Allow people to express their anger.** This is the best way to defuse the situation. Keep your voice low-pitched, stay in control, and take notes. If appropriate, take responsibility for dealing with the problem

SMOOTHING OUT PROBLEMS IN THE EARLY DAYS

If you find you have some unpleasant surprises to deal with early on, there are a few tips that could help. Whatever the situation, stay calm and smile if you can. Your mood will affect everyone around you. If you remain relaxed, colleagues are much more likely to help you sort out the problem.

- **Pause before you react.** Don't turn a crisis into a catastrophe. There's no need for panic. Urgent problems can often be solved quite quickly. But first of all, get to the bottom of it. Find out exactly what is happening. You may not have had the full story from the person who first told you about it. Ask questions
- **Use your head.** Have you ever been in a similar situation? How did you handle it? If you coped before,

you can almost certainly do so again. The same solution may work this time, or you may have to get creative
- **Create some space to deal with the problem if necessary.** Cancel meetings so that you have some spare capacity. Don't add to your problems by failing to turn up to an appointment. If there are other people involved who could make the situation even more difficult, deal with them quickly but firmly
- **Relish the unexpected.** Rise to the challenge of dealing with a problematic situation. In your old job you may not have had such an opportunity. See this as an exciting aspect of your new role as New Kid and "smooth operator." If you're completely stuck, think of someone you admire or respect—tap into your virtual team for help. Ask their advice—what would they do in the circumstances?

DEALING WITH CRITICISM

> When you are being "got at" by someone, it's best to keep your cool. If you can listen without being defensive or showing any negative emotions, you'll make things easier for yourself.

Used wisely, listening skills, like all communication skills, can help defuse the most awkward situations:
- First of all, outline what the other person has said, to make sure you've understood it correctly

- The more specific the criticism is, the more helpful it is
- Find out, by asking questions, why the other person has formed an unfavorable impression of you

Criticism is rarely groundless, but it can often be exaggerated, especially under the influence of heightened emotions. If you can extract the elements that are useful, the experience can be turned to your advantage, in that it can help you to avoid a recurrence of the situation in the future.

More tips for dealing with criticism:

- **You can always try a bit of flattery!** New Kids can often get away with things that people who have been longer in the job can't. Why not ask those responsible for the criticism for their help? If you seek their advice and make them part of the solution strategy, they're likely to form a favorable impression of you. If handled correctly, they could turn out to be useful allies, influential as mentors, coaches, or references
- **Always think positively.** The people who have criticized you have alerted you to a number of things. They may not realize that they have not only given you free information but also enhanced your knowledge of interdepartmental relationships. This will help you to improve your survival strategy and future planning. And by implementing a solution, you take positive steps to avoid similar situations occurring in the future and to improve relationships with colleagues

- **Wherever possible, give praise.** Whether it's other colleagues who help you sort out the problem or those responsible for the criticism, take time to say "thank you". By praising others for their contribution, you will expertly disarm your critics and reinforce the message that this New Kid's behavior in difficult circumstances is exemplary

RESPECT AND TRUST

The establishment of respect and trust in new work relationships is paramount, and here your ability to keep promises speaks volumes. Whether it's about keeping to time, returning calls, providing promised information, or working to agreed budgets, you need to be consistent and not let anyone down in these first few weeks.

It's when trust wavers that relationships with colleagues become shaky. If they can't rely on you, you won't be able to rely on them. Never make claims about your professional ability that you don't believe yourself or can't deliver. No wonder being a New Kid is such hard work. You'll get there—but remember, Rome wasn't built in a day. Nothing worth doing is achieved overnight.

> If you want to convince people of your trustworthiness, you'll need to reassure them that your motives are not self-centered. Self-absorption can wreck the start of many promising working relationships.

Don't put yourself before the needs of your colleagues or boss. Arrogance, ego, and the desire to prove yourself right will work against you. New Kids must remember that self comes last here. Your pursuit of a relationship should be for the other person's benefit in the first place. Once they believe this, you'll gain from it. Remember to be a "giver" rather than a "taker."

Essential to trust is transparency—make your objectives clear and understandable. Otherwise your colleagues won't know how best to help you.

Checklist for developing relationships that work:
- Be transparent in your actions
- Communicate with all sides as well as upward and downward
- Network extensively to keep well-informed
- Identify and watch the "politicians"
- Put yourself in other people's shoes
- Anticipate and manage others' reactions

STEP 09

Big Stick Or Kid Gloves? Dealing With Problems, Laying Down The Law (If Necessary), And The Right Approach To Disciplining Staff

> **❝** I don't know the key to success, but the key to failure is to try to please everybody. **❞**
> *Bill Cosby*

ASSESSING THE SITUATION

How are you getting on? Is the New Kid coping OK? Are you over-subscribing to "office positivism"? This is where, whenever anyone asks you how you're doing, you reply, "Fine," in an upbeat tone, regardless of whether you are or not. How many times have you nodded your head and said you're OK since taking this new job? Are you really coping well or are you secretly feeling that you're struggling to keep on track?

Let's hope it's the former! If, however, you're saying, "Fine," and putting on a brave face, a little self-analysis may perhaps be required. An interesting definition of the word "fine" (not technically accurate but nevertheless amusing) goes like this. Never as a New Kid tell anyone that you're **F I N E**—it means:

- **F**rantic
- **I**nsecure
- **N**eurotic
- **E**motional

So beware: when one of your staff tells you, "I'm fine," it pays to look beneath the surface. They too may be putting on a brave face, and as New Kid manager it's your responsibility to spot any symptoms of distress. Unhealthy suppression of feelings can lead to huge problems, not only for the person in question, but also for colleagues, superiors, and the organization as a whole.

SPOTTING POTENTIAL PROBLEMS
Of course a new job is stressful. In those first few days and weeks there is so much to take on board. Your learning curve is at its steepest and it looks as though you'll never reach cruising altitude. As you know, such feelings are quite normal, yet it pays to be aware of potential trouble spots before they get serious. Better to deal with something while it's still only a glitch, rather than let it reach the problem stage. Never allow a situation to get to crisis point.

As New Kid manager, try to make sense of the whole picture, and get the problem in perspective. For instance, are you looking at it from your own point of view or from that of your staff? If you're concerned, speak to those around you. They'll have their own take on things, and may shrug it off as "the norm." Whatever the case, if you find others have the same view of a situation as you, you'll feel much better.

When facing difficulties in your new job, you as New Kid will come through current turbulence and emerge stronger and more resilient if you keep your cool and remain optimistic and focused. You must celebrate your successes—particularly in the early days, however minor they are—either publicly or in private. Even the most driven people gain strength from taking time to reflect on what they've achieved.

New Kid managers should recognize that what looks like a problem may in fact be an ordinary part of the job. You'll have to deal with unhappy staff, win around obstinate cynics, and listen patiently to unreasonable bosses. This isn't bad luck and you're not being singled out. If you can rise to these challenges and come to regard them as part of the package, you're more likely to cope well.

> Kylie remembers being New Kid manager at a company she took over (management buy-out) some years ago. "The first thing," she says, "was to concentrate on everyone's perception of me, whether they were staff or clients. This was far more important than actually taking time to settle myself in.
>
> "A very enjoyable event on my first day was firing one of the receptionists! She had been consistently rude and dismissive of me when I'd come in under cover to check out the premises and the business.
>
> "I was lucky in that I'd been a client of the business before, so I really knew the ins and outs—certainly from a client perspective. That knowledge helped me a great deal in the early days. I also vaguely knew one of the office managers. She was incredibly helpful, and overjoyed that someone cared about the business and had come along prepared to do something. I took a particular interest in her, was grateful for her support,

> and wanted to help. I was able to promote her quickly; she became my No. 2—a decision I never regretted, even though it was done in relative haste—almost as quickly as the dismissal.
>
> "I recall being extremely nervous for my first few days, which may seem strange considering I was the boss and the owner too. But I was worrying as much about coming in to work as all the staff. I guess that just showed through and made me seem sympathetic. I'm glad I did make the decision to buy the business. It has taken off, been very successful, and I've been rewarded with a group of immensely loyal staff."

Remember—no stress, no success. Appreciate that stress is essential if you're on the way up. You could ask yourself the following questions, or direct them to a member of staff you may be worried about:

- Are you enjoying your work?
- Are you keeping up with developments in your field?
- Are you able to get through what is expected of you on a weekly basis?
- Are you satisfied with the rewards you receive for your efforts and contribution?
- Do you enjoy good relationships with your colleagues, superiors, and staff?
- Do you generally feel in control of your work?
- Are you able to get back on track quickly if problems or crises occur?

If the answers to these questions have mostly been yes, then you've nothing to worry about. New Kids should note that the higher the number of negatives, the more likely there is to be a problem.

Whether this exercise has been directed at yourself or at a member of staff, keep a watching brief to monitor the situation. If when reviewing it you find that the negatives have increased, you should take appropriate measures to bring about a solution. The happier you and your staff are at work, the less harassed you'll be. If your job says something about "who you are," you're probably doing well. If you take pride in your work, the chances are that your job satisfaction levels are high.

When dealing with staff, New Kid managers must apply the same thinking:

- Do your staff feel that the job they are doing is worth while?
- Are they making a real contribution to the workplace?
- Does anyone notice or care? (As New Kid manager, you should.)

Job satisfaction among staff coupled with a supportive working structure and reasonable flexibility will mean that as New Kid manager you're running a good team and keeping control.

If you think one of your staff is not performing well, you should monitor the situation for a short time and then have an informal chat with them, during which you should elicit the following information:

- Are they in control?
- Are they able to delegate?
- Are they being honest with themselves and with you?
- Do they trust their colleagues and superiors?
- Do they actually want to work with others, with you, and with the organization?

Again, the important thing to note here is the number of negatives you end up with. The higher it is, the more serious the potential problem. It could be related to stress, or to performance. And whichever it is, the New Kid manager will need to come up with a remedy—sooner rather than later.

HITTING A ROCKY PATCH

If a member of staff is facing a tough situation, and you as New Kid manager need to help them through, here are some options:

- Observe how other colleagues cope
- If they appear to be doing well, ask them how they manage
- Try to encourage the underachieving staff member to think positively
- Don't assume that a pay raise alone will solve the problem, even if it appears to be money-related
- Help them to stay calm and focused and be supportive
- Reward their effort if appropriate

COPING WITH JEALOUSY IN THE WORKPLACE

> Jeet recalls a significant aspect of taking up his last New Kid position with a government department. He had to deal with varying degrees of resentment expressed (or implied) by several people who thought the job should have been theirs. "It becomes even more complicated," he said, "when more than one colleague feels that way!" He was in a position where he had to rely on them and so could not afford to alienate them, but at the same time had to deal with their negativity.

What if you, as New Kid, experience envy and resentment from your colleagues instead of encouragement and support? Job jealousy abounds and you may come up against a colleague who is trying to cut you down as you are trying to make your mark.

It's a good plan to try to understand the other person's thinking. Are they resentful toward you because of your position? Maybe they'd hoped to get the position themselves? Is it that you're popular and polished while they are not? Or is there another reason? Perhaps they imagine the workplace to be fiercely competitive with only one winner. If you are perceived by them to be gaining the higher ground, their only way to cope is to push themselves forward and try to hold you back.

If it becomes evident that where this person is concerned important phone messages are "forgotten," a piece of must-have information is "mislaid," or perhaps an invitation to a corporate event is "accidentally" deleted, then be alert. Watch out for criticism of your work, and should any of your achievements be slighted, or other forms of unpleasantness occur, it will be time to take counter-measures.

> **!** New Kids should develop a thick skin when starting a new job. But when dealing with the green-eyed monster, don't rise to the bait or retaliate in a similar way. That will only make things worse.

One way to tackle the situation is head-on. Initiate a one-on-one chat, even if you have to persist to get the other person to agree. If you're refused, don't be put off—be tenacious. Open the conversation with something along the lines of "I feel there's some tension between us, and would like us to be able to work well together. Is everything all right?" Or if that's too general, be more assertive, and explain that when the person does X, it makes the working situation difficult, and you'd prefer it if they did Y. End the conversation on a positive note, such as, "Are you OK with this? Is that all right?"

Of course, if the job jealousy persists you'll have to get official and lodge a complaint. This could mean taking disciplinary measures against the person concerned and such processes take time. Whatever course of action you decide on, remaining professional is essential for any New Kid, because you'll have to see the situation through.

DEALING WITH POOR PERFORMANCE

This is something that New Kid managers will have to do from time to time. If staff performance is poor, you have only a few options:

- Put up with it (not recommended)
- Rebrief or retrain to allow performance to improve
- Reassign the person to something they can do
- Terminate employment

These options are linked. For example, you should fire someone only once you've made sure they're in a position to be able to do what it is they're failing to do, and have provided training to help them improve. If no improvement then occurs, more drastic action may be necessary and justified.

> **Don't put off taking action because you're worried about the reaction of others. Provided action is justified, it will almost certainly be approved.**

Most team members hate "passengers" and are conscious that they and their colleagues have to make up the difference. In other words, decisive action in relation to members of the team who are letting the others down will earn you respect.

Sometimes New Kid managers face awkward, contentious, or embarrassing issues—hopefully not in the first few days of their new job, though it has been known to occur! As we've already noted, difficult situations don't get easier if postponed or ignored. In your new position dealing successfully with such situations may be important to your career progress.

New Kids will be under scrutiny during their first few weeks. Everyone will be interested to know how you'll perform "under pressure." What happens if someone makes a stand against you? The simple answer is to show them.

You may do better if you pick your ground, and find a means of demonstrating, early on, that you do have clout and are prepared to use swift and effective measures to sort things out. So:

- Pick a suitable issue (something that matters, but which you're sure of)
- Make a stand, be adamant—explain, by all means, but stick to your guns
- Do not back down (it may well be that pressure to do so at this stage is part of the test)
- Let the word go around—"this one's no soft touch"

MATTERS OF DISCIPLINE

> **!** Never duck or delay matters of staff discipline.

Wouldn't it be wonderful if your staff worked harmoniously and efficiently all of the time? If they never complained, went sick, or had "attitude"? Can you imagine it? Your department fully staffed with "Stepford wife"-type employees? It must surely be every New Kid manager's dream!

The reality is of course somewhat different. People are fallible, staff do make mistakes. Bullying, harassment, and discrimination in the workplace do occur, even in the best companies. Unfortunately, it's usually the job of the manager to sort out the problem, and your new job could involve having to deal with such situations.

New Kid managers know that staff become accountable when they accept an offer of employment. They are required by their contracts to maintain the standards of work and behavior set out in their job descriptions and company code of practice. If they trip up once or twice, perhaps a gentle reminder from a New Kid manager is all that's required.

But if they fail to do what's expected of them on a regular basis, what then? In such circumstances, there are several adverse effects for the company that have to be addressed by the New Kid manager—fast:

- It costs the company money
- It upsets the balance of the workforce ("If they can get away with it, why can't I?")
- Morale plummets
- Management headaches reach epic proportions

Matters of staff discipline have to be tackled urgently, so:

- Check the facts of the case very carefully
- If facts are not clear, check further, but don't delay for too long and set a specific time for further action
- Deal with the matter of itself (don't feel you have to be lenient because it's Day One of your new job)
- Check any planned action against policy (e.g. if a warning is necessary, should it be in writing, how should it be expressed, where should it be filed, and to whom should it be copied?)
- Remember, the key task is to secure the future
- Be fair and don't go over the top in an attempt to register your power

Appropriate action is likely to be approved by the team. Being seen as a soft-touch New Kid can create problems for the future.

MISCONDUCT OR BULLYING

Nowadays, all workers are entitled to be treated with dignity and respect. Bullying, harassment, and discrimination are in no one's interests and New Kid managers should not tolerate them in the workplace. If there are any signs of aggressive behavior, it's essential for New Kid managers to intervene immediately.

Bullying is usually characterized as offensive, intimidating, malicious, or insulting behavior. Harassment is generally unwelcome conduct affecting the dignity of men and women. Discrimination can relate to age, sex, race, disability, religion, nationality, or any personal characteristic of the individual.

If prevention is better than a cure, one good rule for the New Kid manager is to give staff clear examples of what is regarded as unacceptable behavior. You should at an early stage ask the HR department for details of the company's policies and procedures for dealing with grievance and disciplinary matters. Make yourself familiar with these, and, if necessary, ask others in your peer group about past incidents and their outcomes.

As New Kid manager, you should ensure that your staff know to whom they can turn if they have a work-related problem. Make sure that you've received training in all aspects of the organization's policies in this sensitive area.

If this is your first experience of dealing with such issues, it may appear to you that the member of staff who is being bullied or harassed is overreacting to something fairly trivial. Don't judge the situation from your own viewpoint. It could be that this is the "last straw" for your member of staff after a long series of unreported incidents.

The danger for any New Kid manager who allows such behavior to go unchecked is that it creates serious problems

for the organization as a whole. These include:
- Poor morale
- Inharmonious employee relations
- Loss of respect for management
- Bad performance
- Low productivity
- Absences
- Resignations

All of these seriously damage not only your standing within the organization but also the company's reputation.

> New Kid managers should pay close attention to all staff behavior from Day One. You'll never have a better opportunity to study every aspect of the workings of your department than when you first take up your post.

POOR PERFORMANCE

Should you discover that a member of staff makes frequent mistakes, exhibits inappropriate behavior, or performs to standards that fall way short of the company policy, this is not acceptable. They are showing contempt for you and for the company by not caring about their work or their behavior. The effect this has on the organization and the impact of their behavior on their colleagues are detrimental. Swift corrective action needs to be taken by you.

"Why bother?" you may ask. Why risk ending up in front

of an employment tribunal, with all the associated hassle and trauma? After all, it's surely no bad thing to take the ostrich approach (head in sand) and hope matters improve. Isn't it just easier to leave things as they are? Well, actually, it isn't.

ADDRESSING THE PROBLEM

New Kid managers know that no problem ever got smaller by being left alone. What starts as a minor dispute can quickly develop into a full-blown crisis if ignored. If an issue is not confronted, things will only get worse.

> Don't confuse discipline with punishment. Discipline is positive; punishing someone entails exacting a penalty.

Effective discipline involves dealing with someone's shortcomings or misconduct before the problem escalates. Depending on the severity of the problem, disciplining an employee can be an informal or formal procedure. If an informal approach is appropriate, counseling or training can play a vital part in resolving complaints.

Whichever the case, it's important that New Kid managers follow a fair procedure. When the issue involves a complaint about bullying, harassment, or discrimination, there must be fairness to both the complainant and the person accused.

It's essential for New Kid managers to set a good example. The faster you deal with the problem, the stronger example of management you are giving. If you allow time to elapse between the incident itself and the disciplining of the staff member, the message you are sending is weak—that you couldn't be bothered to do much about it.

You must maintain fair procedures for dealing promptly with complaints from staff. In most organizations, standards of behavior are set by means of a statement given to all staff when they join or through the company handbook.

As New Kid manager you should make it clear to all your staff that any complaints of bullying, harassment, or discrimination will be dealt with fairly, confidentially, and sensitively, as laid down in the company manual.

SUGGESTED COURSE OF ACTION

First of all, identify the problem. It's important to find out whether the issue you are dealing with is related to performance or misconduct. Then:

- Try to deal with the matter as quickly as possible
- Make sure you explain why the individual is being disciplined
- Describe exactly what the unacceptable behavior is (it's essential to avoid generalities here—be as specific as possible)
- Stick to the facts—focus on the behavior and not the person
- Explain the effect their behavior is having on the rest of the unit/department/company
- Specify what changes need to be made

- Outline what will happen if the unacceptable behavior continues

In order to comply with the law, which requires fairness above all things, New Kid managers need to carry out a full investigation, giving the individual the opportunity to state their case. The party under investigation is allowed to be accompanied to any interview or hearing by a representative or colleague. New Kid managers must give an explanation for the disciplinary action and describe the appeals procedure.

It's very difficult for anyone, whether new to a post or experienced, to deal with a situation where they suspect that someone has made an unfounded allegation of bullying, harassment, or discrimination for malicious reasons. In such instances, it's essential that the allegation is fully investigated and dealt with fairly and objectively through the disciplinary procedure.

Depending on the outcome of the procedure, New Kid managers should take reasonable action in relation to the facts. Penalties are not always necessary. As mentioned above, it may be more appropriate to offer counseling or training. In the severest cases, where bullying, harassment, or discrimination amounts to gross misconduct, dismissal without notice may be the right course of action.

Where such issues arise, New Kid managers should seek advice from their HR or legal department, as company policies, procedures, and working methods may need to be improved.

> **When taking action involving personnel, you can't have too much documentation.**

Should you ever have to discipline a member of your staff, remember the golden rule: **Keep a record of everything**.

- Give fair warning (along with notification of the consequences of non-compliance)
- Give your member of staff enough time to respond, or to rectify their behavior
- Make sure your company's policies are reasonable
- Be clear what avenues there are for appeal and describe them to the member of staff

The law in this area is complicated, and you should consult your company's legal department for specific advice.

> Hard work spotlights the character of people: some turn up their sleeves, some turn up their noses, and some don't turn up at all.
>
> *Sam Ewing*

STEP 10

If It Ain't Broke, Don't Fix It: Maintaining Performance And Ongoing Development

> **❝** Even if you're on the right track, you'll get run over if you just sit there. **❞**
>
> *Arthur Godfrey*

Getting things done—that's what New Kids want to feel they're doing. Everyone who has been a New Kid at some time or other remembers the terrible feelings of inadequacy and frustration they had during those first few days and weeks in their new job.

So, how far can you go when taking over a job as New Kid manager? How long before you need to make your mark? Don't move too fast—get the lie of the land. It's usual to give yourself at least 90 days to assess the situation, understand the politics, and make sure you fully appreciate the issues.

Jake joined a new company—it was his first appointment as senior manager—and made the mistake of attempting to introduce changes on several fronts at the same time. The result: he undermined the other managers around him, generated mistrust, and ultimately set in train actions that took almost a year to reverse. The lesson Jake learned: "You have two ears and one mouth—best to use them in that proportion."

NOTHING IS FOR EVER

For New Kids, change and new challenges are the order of the day. You may not know what's coming, but during the first few weeks of your new job you'll experience a lot of new things and will need help and support from colleagues and staff to get you through.

All action you take early on in your job must be predicated on the necessity not only of creating an effective relationship with your staff and colleagues but also of maintaining it. There are two things you need to consider alongside each other:

THE SHORT TERM
- What will be the immediate impact of what you instigate?
- How will people respond?
- How will it add to the growing view people have of you as New Kid?
- Will it prove to be effective?

THE LONG TERM
- Does what you are doing set an unfortunate precedent?
- Is this an approach that makes long-term sense?

> **!** If an action that you have to take now causes an upset, ask yourself whether the logic of it will perhaps be clear later on. It's always wise to keep the long term in mind.

As New Kid manager, your job is to get things done and to achieve your objectives. Doing this demands that you win—and retain—the goodwill and support of your team. On an ongoing basis, you'll do well to consider:
- The effectiveness of your decision and actions
- How they're perceived by others

If the response is positive, people will approve the decision and applaud you for the line you've taken. If you feel the response is negative, you may need to:
- Reconsider your decision and select another way forward
- Go ahead with your chosen course of action, but explain why this particular approach is necessary
- Compensate for the negative reaction in some way

MAINTAINING CREDIBILITY
If as New Kid you act as you mean to go on, people will believe in you and respect what you do. Remember:
- You are judged not by the number of times you fail, but by the number of your successes—keep an eye on the ratio
- You are more likely to succeed by sticking your neck out than by always playing it safe
- If you admit your mistakes, people will see you are human, and will help you not to repeat them (and will avoid making similar ones themselves)
- Never close off an option before you have to—you may find you need it later on

> **! New Kids should aim to create a persona that inspires respect and confidence. Remember that your success can rub off on others.**

There's one maxim that all frustrated New Kids should bear in mind. It's simply this: New Kids cannot have instant power and credit.

It takes time to make your mark. You'll have to be patient, because, for a while at least, you'll be dependent to some extent on the rest of your team or department. While you may have the power to get things done, as a New Kid you cannot go it alone, but will have to enlist their help.

As long as this is the case, you must give other people credit for what they do. Never:

- Pass off their ideas as yours (even when you've contributed to them)
- Talk about "what I've done" when you mean what "we" or better still "they" have done
- Fail actively to give credit, both within the group and beyond

New Kid, your success depends on the support of your colleagues. If you take credit for what they do, they'll resent it—and rightly so.

This will adversely affect their performance and reflect badly on you. If you want credit, it must come from what you as New Kid do to enhance the performance of your team or department.

YOUR STYLE OF MANAGEMENT

If you're a New Kid manager, whatever processes you set up will be seen as a sign of your style. If they're approved, they'll build trust. If not, they'll distance you from your staff.

Overall, New Kids must make sure that their systems and processes are:

- Fair
- Relevant
- Effective
- Understandable
- Time-(and cost-) effective

And that they're not:

- Bureaucratic
- Restrictive
- Contradictory
- Out of touch with reality
- Incompatible with other systems (or common sense)
- Over-complex

Everything you set up (or maintain, if it was set up by someone else) must help your section to be effective and efficient. If you introduce inappropriate systems, those who do the work will quickly come to see you as someone who is making their job more difficult.

WHO CALLS THE SHOTS?

If you're a New Kid in charge, make this clear. You may be

new, and you may depend to some extent on the support of your colleagues, but you call the shots. The hierarchy means something and you should not apologize for it.

Supervision works best when it's not overt. You may feel somewhat inadequate about supervising as New Kid, when almost all your staff know more about the company (and your job) than you do, but ultimately you must supervise, and this means:

- Making it clear on what issues your approval is required and how it should be sought
- Keeping control of key issues, but thinking carefully about what they are and where you can empower people to make their own decisions
- Recognizing that the buck stops with you, facing issues, making decisions, and never saying you'll deal with something and then sidelining or endlessly postponing it
- Being prepared to stick your neck out at times and always having the courage of your convictions

> Your staff must never doubt who is in charge. Remember that if you look like a doormat, even for a second, people will walk all over you. Once lost, credibility is hard to win back.

TRAINING AND DEVELOPMENT

Staff development is sufficiently important to people (as well as being important in its own right) for it to be worth your while to address it straightaway and give out the right messages early on.

You may sensibly decide not to send everyone off on a course in your first week. But there are other things you might consider, such as asking:

- Should development be on the agenda for meetings?
- Can any form of development be undertaken "on the job"?
- Can any ongoing development be instigated now?

An organization's attitude to training and development is important to its staff. In part the view they take is dependent on you, as New Kid manager. Send the right signals.

ONGOING DEVELOPMENT

Nothing is so important to people as their success. Time and again you hear people say, for example, "Above all, I want to work with people from whom I can learn." Your own development as New Kid, together with that of your staff, is something you should not ignore, nor should you leave it to the training department. The responsibility is yours.

You should aim to make sure your staff have the knowledge, skills, and attitudes needed to do their jobs—and to do them well. Development is not just about correcting weaknesses. It's about upgrading and taking people forward, not least to keep up with change.

Your staff must see that you:
- Recognize that their development is important
- Intend to help them gain experience and extend their skills

- Are creating a system by which to do so

Use the development cycle to help you:
- Analyze the job (what does it require?)
- Analyze the person (what competencies do they have?)
- Look ahead: anticipate what new skills the job might require in the future
- Define the skills "gap"—what must be done to create a good fit between the person and the job
- Specify development activity, methods, budget, and priorities
- Implement action and monitor results

This is a rolling cycle. Keep clear records, make sure everyone is reviewed in this way, and create a culture in which people value development and what it brings.

APPRAISALS

As New Kid manager, you may be responsible for conducting annual appraisals of your staff. If so, in order to make it a productive experience for both sides, think seriously about the questions you're going to ask.

They should include the following:
- Where does the staff member in question fit in the company hierarchy?
- What is their current role and what are the main tasks associated with it?
- What difficulties do they face and what do they consider to be the solutions?

- What are their greatest accomplishments?
- Where do they want to go?
- How could they get there?
- What makes them different from their peers?

If the person undergoing appraisal doesn't moan about their position but rather suggests solutions to problems, this is constructive. If you also hear a reasoned response in answer to criticism of performance, this information is important. The purpose of an appraisal is to clarify for both parties what is expected of the staff member in the future and what support they can expect from you in return.

> Part of your job is helping people to learn. But as a responsible New Kid manager, you also have a responsibility toward yourself.

TAKING SIDES

As a New Kid you have a juggling act to perform, one that balances different points of view; these are essentially those of:
- Yourself
- The organization
- Your department/section
- Your staff
- External contacts (customers, suppliers)

There are often conflicts here. Something may be right for the department and the staff, but not for the organization or for you. New Kids will find themselves in the position of disagreeing with a policy but having to support it.

So how do you handle this balancing act? Keep the following in mind:

- Your responsibility is first to the organization and the results you are charged with producing
- You can only produce these results with support from your staff, so you must carry them with you
- You have a responsibility both upward and downward within the organization
- You must never be seen to be selfish, or as if you are acting simply to make things easier for yourself
- You must sometimes be seen to be fighting your corner on behalf of your section

Everyone is capable of getting what they really want out of life, provided they know which way they want to go. Energy and motivation are the currency needed to manage the process of change in the workplace. In terms of career management and self-development, change is a constant part of life.

ADVANCING YOUR CAREER

You have just achieved a step up the career ladder—you're a New Kid, glowing with pride. With all this positive change, how can you ensure that you'll continue to develop, make better choices, manage your career while getting satisfaction from your role as New Kid?

First, keep the key functions in mind:
- Define your objectives
- Plan (and allocate a time to) your actions
- Communicate (throughout the process)
- Support the actions of others
- Evaluate performance (and link to the future)

It's important at the outset to take a long, hard look at yourself. You must know your strengths and weaknesses. Provided you know what they are, you can play to your strengths and work on your weaknesses.

One advantage of working in teams when you're a New Kid is that you can initially get colleagues to compensate for what you're not good at. But you should assume the role of your own champion where professional development is concerned. Being proactive helps—it's no longer enough to be hardworking and hope that someone notices you. You need to manage your profile, identify stakeholders who can help you with your career advancement.

It's important to give yourself regular reviews to ensure that your career is heading in the right direction. Remember to enjoy your new position and start taking pride in your achievements.

DIY PERSONAL DEVELOPMENT

So, here is your "design it yourself" course in personal development. The major questions you'll need to consider may be divided into sections:

WHERE YOU ARE NOW
- How challenging is your job?
- Does your work allow you to express yourself and your values?
- What skills would it be wise to upgrade in order to ensure career progression?
- Is anything currently standing in the way of your success?
- If so, what is it, and how will you deal positively with it?

COPING WITH CHANGE
- Can you cope with continual change?
- Do you find change threatening or challenging?
- Are the changes taking place around you positive ones?
- How will you manage those changes for your continued success?
- Are they better for you, or better for the company? (Ideally, they should be both.)

> Avoid getting drawn into areas of change that you can't control. If you think you can have a positive influence, get involved. If you can't, don't waste valuable time and energy.

When change is imposed on you, you have no choice but to accept it. What you can do, however, is choose how you respond to it. If you can develop an "adapt and thrive" approach to change, you'll find that you can manage it positively.

If you know that change is about to occur, it helps to be proactive. Get involved, prepare for the challenges that the change will bring. By welcoming change you'll find that you're able to take advantage of new and better opportunities. This could mean looking at ways of improving your skills, your position within the company, or your relationships within the workplace.

If you can keep up with the changes that surround you and use them as a positive and motivational driver, they'll help you to achieve your goals.

FUTURE PLANNING
- Where do you want to be in five years' time?
- Plan your route—what you need to do, who you need to have with you as part of your team
- Acknowledge every step of your personal achievement
- Continually motivate yourself
- Set goals, remembering that they can sometimes be achieved more quickly by involving others
- Figure out who else needs to be involved
- Take full responsibility for your targets

Personal development means embracing change, and embracing change takes courage, because it involves leaving a situation you're comfortable with. You have to make a conscious decision to step outside of that comfort zone and welcome new challenges.

BUILDING ON SUCCESS

Ongoing success for you, New Kid, involves a cycle of activity:
- Understanding what is essential to success
- Being conscious of how you do things as you do them
- Planning and acting in accordance with that
- Monitoring the results arising from what you do
- Fine-tuning, and building on the experience of how things work to improve what you do next

> ! Never rest on your laurels; remember that even the best performance can be improved upon.

MOVING ON?

A good start is desirable in its own right. Not only does it make for a more comfortable transition for you, but it also brings better results. You've now considered all the aspects of coping with change so, if you've come full circle and you're moving on, you've got the tools you need to make the best of new situations.

Ongoing New Kid success will be influenced by:
- The attitude you take to transition
- What you do before you move into your next New Kid appointment
- The early focus you bring to bear on key issues
- The relationships you cultivate with your boss, colleagues, and staff

- The working habits you create for yourself (and others) during the New Kid period

All of the above influence your early success in the job and the way you take things forward for the future.

> **!** You only get one chance to get off to a good start. Be sure to make the most of it, as it will have an impact for a long time to come.

From the beginning, how to be a great New Kid:
- First organize yourself and then others
- Take your time (you can't achieve miracles in a day)
- Make the effort (no quick fixes or magic formulas)
- Keep thinking (the obvious or immediate answer may not be the best)
- Take advice whenever you can (it's not a solo effort)
- Be prepared to admit your mistakes, publicly if necessary
- Learn from your experiences
- Maintain regular and clear communication

Being an effective New Kid is not so much about what you get people to do as about the process you engage in working with them to help your performance and their development.

> **!** In the end success comes down to a considered approach. Charge in, desperate to make an impression, go at everything at once, and disaster may follow.

Remember: "There are no short cuts to any place worth going to" (Beverley Sills).

Taking on board the suggestions made here will not erase all the pain of being a New Kid on the Block. However, by the end of the first three months in your new job most people will have formed an impression of you that will be hard to change. So, you need to make as good a first impression as possible, which can then be reinforced the more they get to know you. Many things can aid the learning process, but only one person can guarantee that you'll survive and thrive in the first 100 days in your new job, and that's you!

About the Author

FRANCES KAY is a business development consultant who advises successful and fast-growing companies on corporate connections, business introductions and strategic alliances. She also acts as a business coach and course leader.

Her previous books include *Making Management Simple* (with Helen Guinness and Nicola Stevens), *Brilliant Business Connections* and *Kickstart Your Time Management*.